MICHIGAN
MOTIVATIONS

An Imprint of
INDIANA UNIVERSITY PRESS

MICHIGAN
MOTIVATIONS

A YEAR OF INSPIRATION WITH
THE UNIVERSITY OF
MICHIGAN WOLVERINES

CYLE YOUNG
and
DEL DUDUIT

This book is a publication of

Quarry Books
an imprint of

Indiana University Press
Office of Scholarly Publishing
Herman B Wells Library 350
1320 East 10th Street
Bloomington, Indiana 47405 USA

iupress.indiana.edu

© 2020 by Cyle Young and Del Duduit

Manufactured in the United States of America

Cataloging information is available from the Library of Congress.
ISBN 978-0-253-04819-6 (hardback)
ISBN 978-0-253-04820-2 (paperback)
ISBN 978-0-253-04822-6 (ebook)

1 2 3 4 5   25 24 23 22 21 20

CONTENTS

FOREWORD

IN THE BOOK *MICHIGAN MOTIVATIONS*, written by former Michigan football player Cyle Young and his coauthor, Del Duduit, you will find a collection of University of Michigan football stories, including some of the most exciting football games ever played by Wolverine teams across the ages. Not only do Cyle and Del capture the excitement and suspense of each of these historic Michigan football games, they also leave the reader with great inspirational and insightful life lessons that everyone can relate to in their day-to-day victories and losses.

These stories cover the full breadth of the history of Michigan football, from the early days of Michigan's first football teams to Fielding H. Yost's point-a-minute program. This book goes well beyond the introduction of the winged helmet by Fritz Crisler and utilizes pivotal moments in the history of the game to help mold and shape readers into Michigan Men and Women, cut from the same cloth as the likes of Schembechler, Carr, and Harbaugh.

As a player for the University of Michigan, Cyle lived through some of these games and learned firsthand the lessons of life that can come from the football field at U of M and playing on one of the biggest stages in college football today. I love how he recaps two football games that I played in at Michigan, with the 1980 team the 1981 Rose Bowl win (Bo Schembechler's first Bowl win) and the Indiana versus Michigan, John Wangler–to–Anthony Carter, last-second homecoming win in 1979.

Winner of over 950 games and 11 national and 42 conference titles, the University of Michigan football team has left a winning legacy on the field. With the help of *Michigan Motivations*, Wolverine fans can take that same winning legacy into their workplaces, homes, schools, and communities.

Cyle and Del capture the heart of Michigan's classic games! They would have made my old coach Bo Schembechler very proud of this book.

—*George Lilja*

ACKNOWLEDGMENTS

I NEVER WOULD HAVE BEEN able to attend the University of Michigan without the generous love and support of my mother and father. A hearty thanks to Chris and Candice Young, who helped to make me a Michigan Man. Their many sacrifices paved the way for me to play football from an early age all the way through college.

I also want to thank my football coaches who made a lasting impression on my life. Thank you to Pete Gilliam, who helped me learn to love the sport; Shawn Watton, who always pushed me to be better; and Bobby Morrison, who recruited me to Michigan. A final thank you to Coach Brady Hoke, who made four years of Michigan football fun and exciting.

Thank you to my teammates Gary Rose, Brodie Killian, Adam Adkins, and Eric Warner. You were the greatest roommates I could have asked for. And a final thank you to Del Duduit for writing this book with me.

—Cyle

Thank you to my wife, Angie, for your love and encouragement. I'm grateful for the many hours you spend editing my work and thank you for always standing by my side in support as I pursue my love of writing. I couldn't do this without you, and I love you so much.

Thank you to Cyle Young, my agent and coauthor of this book, for working with me on this project. You inspire me to take chances, and I appreciate the many doors you have helped to open for me. It was great to work together with you to make this project happen.

Thank you to Ashley Runyon and Indiana University Press for this exciting opportunity. We appreciate your faith in us as well as your flexibility.

—*Del*

MICHIGAN
MOTIVATIONS

INTRODUCTION

HAIL, MICHIGAN FAN!

What first began as rugby-football has blossomed into an all-encompassing culture. From the handfuls of fans who watched the first football game in 1879 to the hundreds of thousands of Michigan faithful who watch the games today, Michigan has not only stood the test of time, it has come out on top.

The University of Michigan is the winningest program in college football history, and over the years it has created heroes and legends who still motivate and inspire young and old. *Michigan Motivations* tells those stories.

Each week you'll be inspired by some of the legends of the game. Relive the Wolverines' most famous moments and discover how you, too, can overcome adversity, find success, understand true teamwork, and much more. *Michigan Motivations* is for every fan who bleeds Maize and Blue. You'll rejoice in the come-from-behind victories, struggle with surprise losses, and scratch your head at how Ohio State went to the Rose Bowl in 1974.

Michigan's story is every fan's story. Inside these pages, you'll learn how to become a true Michigan Man or Michigan Woman: a person of character and integrity who makes the choices of a valiant victor. A person who not only embraces adversity but always strives to overcome like a conquering hero.

Discover how to climb your own personal Mount Everest like the 1997 Wolverines. Understand how to find personal success at home, at work, at school, or at play. Be challenged to live your life to the fullest as a champion in your home, work, or community.

You'll be inspired by the likes of Tom Harmon, Anthony Carter, Desmond Howard, Charles Woodson, and Tom Brady. You'll appreciate the Wolverine persistence that crafted a 1934 team MVP into the thirty-eighth president for the United States and learn to apply that same Michigan character in your own life.

As a former football player on the 1997–2000 teams, I witnessed a few of these powerful moments from the sidelines. They are still as transformative today as they were live, and the lessons I learned from them stick with me. Reexperience these moments and others and allow them to motivate you to be the best version of yourself—a champion of the West.

Go Blue!

Cyle Young
Michigan Football, Class of 2001

SPRING TRAINING

BE EXTRAORDINARY

Del Duduit

January 1, 1993: Michigan 38, Washington 31

TYRONE WHEATLEY WAS ANYTHING BUT ordinary on this New Year's Day.

The seventy-ninth Rose Bowl featured the seventh-ranked University of Michigan Wolverines against the ninth-ranked University of Washington Huskies in Pasadena, California. The game is still considered one of the greatest contests in Rose Bowl history. It had it all—six lead changes and drama at the end. The fans rose to their feet in anticipation as the Big Ten champion Wolverines scored the final two touchdowns of the game to come from behind for a 38–31 win.

But Michigan's Wheatley was the true hero of the game.

He turned in an amazing performance for the Maize and Blue as he rushed for three touchdowns and piled up 235 yards on the ground. His first score was an all-out 56-yard rumble that boosted his Wolverines to a 10–7 lead. Wheatley's next run was an 88-yard dash that showed why he was an All-American and Big Ten Conference track-and-field sprinter. Next on the agenda was his 24-yard dart in the third quarter. This run was incredible, as he later admitted he had been injured in the second quarter and had numbness in his legs. He played hurt and did not let anyone know; victory meant too much to him.

Wheatley was described as a beast on the football field. He was a tough guy. But he also knew he was not solely responsible for the win. He gave credit to Michigan quarterback Elvis Grbac for leading the team throughout the game.

Washington had beaten Michigan in the Rose Bowl the previous year, and both Grbac and Wheatley were determined it was not going to happen again. For an entire season, the loss in the 1992 Rose Bowl stung and lingered in the back of Wheatley's mind. He drew inspiration and motivation from the loss. The only way to win was to be exceptional.

How do you overcome losses and focus on being exceptional when the odds are stacked against you? Are you able to rally to win the game?

GO FOR THE PYLON

Have you ever dealt with discouragement or loss? Maybe you received a job demotion, or a loved one was sick in the hospital. Or perhaps you messed up and hurt people you love. You don't have to live with a previous defeat to win the game at hand. There are ways to move past failure and be head and shoulders above the rest.

PLAN YOUR DEFENSE

Create and use a day-to-day plan, such as a daily checklist. Knowing what you have to accomplish sets the tone for the day, and you'll get a sense of satisfaction when you cross an item off. Your list may include trivial tasks, such as cleaning the garage, or items of greater concern, such as consoling a friend through a hard time. Whatever you add to your list, make a genuine effort to complete as many tasks as possible.

Keep a daily journal to record the events of your day. You can write paragraphs or just one or two sentences. You might jot down something humorous or of substantial significance. Don't stick to the good news; also take note of mistakes you made. We all make mistakes. But learn from them, and promise never to repeat them.

Don't be afraid to ask for help. Put aside your ego and ask others for assistance when you have a predicament you can't figure out. This is not a sign of weakness but rather of respect. Knowledge is a commodity, and the best way to gain it is to ask questions.

Don't beat yourself up. Success does not happen overnight. Set goals and try to reach them. When you fall short or make a mistake, recognize that you made the effort and keep going. If you dwell on your failures, you won't find the end zone.

Give thanks and smile. A grateful and thankful heart draws people like honey, and a smile is contagious and stimulates a positive attitude. Finally, laugh—especially at yourself. Remarkable people are aware that a life worth living includes plenty of laughter.

Over Wheatley's career, he worked hard at his craft to be the best he could be. You have to do the same throughout your day. You want a life that is captivating and exciting, so go the extra mile and even play when hurt if you must. The point is to enjoy the time you have, because one day the game will be over and you will want to be remembered as someone who never settled for ordinary. God put you here for a reason. Find your purpose, and rumble for three touchdowns. Go Blue!

How can you improve? What list can you make?

_____

_____

_____

_____

_____

_____

_____

_____

_____

_____

_____

_____

_____

_____

_____

_____

_____

_____

_____

_____

_____

_____

_____

_____

_____

_____

ANYTHING IS POSSIBLE

Cyle Young

October 30, 2004: Michigan State at Michigan

MICHIGAN STATE UNIVERSITY'S 4–4 FOOTBALL team rolled into Ann Arbor with a chip on their shoulder. Their twelve previous games at Michigan Stadium had ended in defeat. But after fifty-one minutes of battle, the MSU Spartans stood just under nine minutes from upsetting the 8–1 Michigan Wolverines. Spartan quarterback Drew Stanton had been knocked out of the game late in the first half, but the visiting team held a tight grip on the lead.

The Wolverines found themselves with their backs against the wall. They needed three scores in eight minutes just to tie the game and push it into overtime. But not only did they have to score, they also had to shut down the Spartan offense in the final minutes.

The Wolverines charged down the field with a key 13-yard run by Mike Hart and a 46-yard pass to wide receiver Braylon Edwards. But the drive fell short. The offense stalled and had to settle for a field goal. The resulting 3 points pulled them to within two touchdowns.

On a risky play call, Coach Carr went for an early onside kick. Brian Thompson recovered the kick, giving the Wolverines another chance to bring the game to within 7 points. Edwards and quarterback Chad Henne took over the game. Their performance elevated the entire team, and after a 37-yard touchdown pass, Michigan pulled to within one touchdown.

On the next drive, the Wolverine defense held, but the Spartans had run 2:50 off the clock. Michigan got the ball back, and Henne found Edwards again, this time for a 22-yard touchdown.

Tie game.

Michigan pulled off the impossible, but the Spartans wouldn't go down without a fight. Backup quarterback Damon Dowdell drove MSU down the field for a final field goal attempt with three seconds left. But fate sent the ball wide, and the game went into overtime.

The men of Michigan couldn't give up at the end of regulation. The hard-fought battle wasn't over. No player and no fan would be happy with losing in overtime. The Wolverines had to rally every ounce of effort and continue the improbable come-from-behind victory.

In the first overtime, the teams traded field goals. Double overtime brought a pair of touchdowns and sent the rivalry into its first-ever triple-overtime game. No matter which team came out on top, the game would live in MSU/UM lore for generations. But the Michigan players weren't going to settle. The season was at stake. Their state pride was on the line.

The offense fastened their chinstraps and strutted onto the field to start the third overtime. Henne found

Edwards yet again, giving Edwards his third and final touchdown of the day. Michigan pulled ahead 45–37. If the defense held, sighs of relief would be heard all over the Lower Peninsula.

It did.

Michigan won in triple overtime because they wouldn't give up. They fought until the end. Every coach and every player pulled together for a victory for the ages. Even when the stadium seats had begun to clear early in the fourth quarter because the Wolverines trailed by 17 on their home turf, the team still held together. They wouldn't be deterred, and they wouldn't let the Spartans upset them at home, in front of their crowd.

Have you ever faced almost certain defeat and managed to pull out from behind? Do you have a team you can rely on to push you through to the win?

BEAT THE ODDS

We all go through times in life like this. Sometimes when we expect things to be an easy success, they just don't go our way. A surefire win can easily be clouded by a potential defeat at home, at work, and in other areas of your life.

But you can overcome an adversary and have the final victory. Whether your struggle is against a person or a situation, you can get back in the game. Even if the odds seem like they are stacked against you, there's always the possibility for success if you are willing to work hard, fight hard, and overcome. But remember, the victory may not come easily. You might have to win it in the third overtime.

MOVE ONWARD TOWARD VICTORY

Fasten your chinstrap: Get back in the game! If you feel that the odds are against you at home, at work, or in life, take a deep breath, swallow your pride, and take your first step toward victory. You can overcome!

Ignore the doubters: When winning becomes an uphill battle, the doubters will be standing at the ready to watch you fail. Your true fans—your spouse, your children, your extended family, and your truest friends—will be waiting to support and celebrate your success. They will always believe in you, so you should believe in yourself also. Go Blue!

What do you need to overcome? Who will be there to help you win?

_____

_____

_____

_____

_____

_____

_____

_____

_____

_____

_____

_____

_____

_____

_____

_____

CARRY THE LOAD

Del Duduit

October 10, 1981: Michigan 38, Michigan State 20

MICHIGAN WAS DOWN 20–16 IN the third quarter to unranked Michigan State.

Both teams were playing for the honor of winning the Paul Bunyan Trophy, which had been a tradition since 1953. The trophy is a large, four-foot-tall wooden statue of legendary lumberjack Paul Bunyan that sits upon a five-foot base. The trophy design is in recognition of the state's history as a producer of lumber products.

The Wolverines entered the contest 3–1, while the Spartans struggled to have a 1–3 record. A win over Michigan on the Spartans' home turf would make up for their slow start.

But Maize and Blue running back Butch Woolfolk made sure that did not happen. He led a comeback in the second half, and Michigan whipped off 22 unanswered points to win the game 38–20.

Woolfolk enjoyed the best game of his storied career. He carried the ball an impressive thirty-nine times for 253 yards. After the game, Wolverine coach Bo

Schembechler, who had a hot-and-cold relationship with his player, called him one of the best backs in school history.

And it came as no surprise. Woolfolk started the season in 1981 with five straight games of 100 or more yards. He led Michigan to a 9–3 season and a 33–14 Bluebonnet Bowl win over UCLA. In that game, he gained 186 yards in the victory and was named Most Valuable Player. Although he was awarded the game's highest honor, he said the only thing he would remember about the contest was that it was his last game as a Wolverine.

For three consecutive seasons, Woolfolk was the team's leading rusher. During his sophomore year, he earned 990 yards. The following season, he tallied 1,042 yards with eight touchdowns. But in his final year, he blazed the ground for 1,459 yards. On average, he gained an astonishing 5.2 yards per carry.

Woolfolk was known as a power runner, but he also whipped off long gains. Such was the case in 1979 when he darted 92 yards against Wisconsin. Two years later, he bolted 89 yards, again against the Badgers.

Woolfolk was an All-American in 1981 and first team All-Big Ten for three years. He also won the Rose Bowl MVP in January 1981 when Michigan defeated the University of Washington Huskies 23–6.

Woolfolk was a workhorse who carried the load for his team. He ran with a mission and got the job done.

Do you pull your weight around your home or workplace? Do you operate as a team player?

REVIEW THE PLAYBOOK

Are there areas in your life where you can make some adjustments? Perhaps you tend to complain about situations instead of focusing on the positive. Maybe you shift blame to others when unpleasant circumstances arise. You are human, and it's easy to point a finger, especially if you are not the one who made a wrong decision. But your actions and attitude can have an impact on those around you. Do you add to their burden, or do you help lighten their load?

CARRY THE LOAD

You may never get the opportunity to run for 253 yards against one of your rivals, but you can carry the load in your own way for those who depend on you. It all boils down to taking responsibility and doing what is expected of you.

The first step is to own your thoughts, actions, and words. You alone have the ability to control your thoughts and what comes out of your mouth. Be a good role model and talk like an adult. Never blame others for your actions. When you push responsibility to a family member or a business partner, you set yourself up as the victim, which lessens the chances of changing your situation. When you take ownership, you put yourself in a position to make alterations.

You can also carry the load when you stop complaining. When an event that is out of your control and impacts you in a negative way takes place, try to look at the big picture and learn from the situation. Perhaps one of the biggest challenges in taking on responsibility is to not take things personally. Most of the time, circumstances are not about you but about others. Think about ways you can make a difference. Always demonstrate good intentions, live in the present and not the past, and be happy. When you do these things, you will carry the load for those around you. You will look for the good in people and be more enjoyable to be around. Go Blue!

How do you contribute at home or at work? Do you carry your load?

_____

_____

_____

_____

_____

_____

_____

_____

_____

_____

_____

_____

_____

_____

_____

_____

_____

_____

_____

_____

_____

_____

_____

_____

_____

_____

_____

LITTLE BROTHER

Cyle Young

November 3, 2007: Michigan at Michigan State

THE 2007 SEASON WAS SUPPOSED to be great. University of Michigan entered the season ranked number five in the country. The nation expected Michigan, with a large group of returning players, to be one of the teams to beat. However, after humiliating losses to University of Oregon and Appalachian State, Michigan had slipped from frontrunner to disappointment.

A late-season meeting between Michigan and in-state rival Michigan State would make or break the season for both teams. After the rough start to the season, Michigan had managed to win seven straight games and brought a 7–2 record into the rivalry game. Michigan State struggled through their first season with new head coach Mark Dantonio. The team's 5–4 record was nothing to be excited about, but a victory over Michigan would end the Spartans' season on a high note.

As with any UM and MSU game, players on both teams traded barbs via the media. Anticipation built in the weeks leading up to the game, and even though neither team entered the game with a championship-caliber season, in-state bragging rights were on the line.

In the first half, everything pointed to an easy Wolverine victory. Spartan quarterback Brian Hoyer struggled to find wide-open receivers. With the Spartans' obvious offensive challenges, the Wolverines managed to take a 14–3 lead into halftime. The MSU cornerbacks struggled to contain Michigan's star receiver, Mario Manningham, who would finish the game with eight receptions for 129 yards.

At halftime, the teams entered their respective locker rooms to game-plan for the second half. When the Spartans returned to the field, they looked like a completely different team. At the close of the third quarter, running back Javon Ringer ripped off a 72-yard run to set up Brian Hoyer's go-ahead touchdown pass, and giving the Spartans a 17–14 lead. Shortly after, running back Jehuu Caulcrick converted a 1-yard rush for a touchdown to give MSU a 24–14 lead with 7:40 left in the game.

Michigan had to get their act together fast. On the next drive, Wolverine quarterback Chad Henne twisted his ankle. He had to leave the field for one play, and freshman quarterback Ryan Mallett replaced him on the field. Mallett fumbled the snap, but running back Mike Hart grabbed the ball and ran for a first down. MSU coach Dantonio later stated, "The turning point was when the ball came out and we blitzed Mallett, and Hart scooped it up."

And a turning point it was.

Henne reentered the game on the next play and ended that drive with a touchdown pass to Greg Matthews. Only forty-eight seconds had expired since the Spartans had scored.

Michigan's defense held on the Spartans' next possession, and the Wolverine offense entered the field with
momentum. Henne drove Michigan down the field and
on third and eleven tossed the game-winning pass to
Manningham.

After the game, Michigan running back Hart famously
quipped, "Sometimes you get your little brother excited
when you're playing basketball—let them get the lead.
And then you come back." This come-from-behind victory didn't only help Michigan recover some pride in
its season, it also created the new MSU moniker "Little
Brother," which is still in use by UM fans today.

Have you ever faced what you thought were unbeatable
odds and pulled out a win anyway? How were you able to
push yourself to victory?

COME FROM BEHIND

The early season losses were devastating for the Wolverines, but the team didn't let them ruin their season. Sure,
Oregon and Appalachian State were major setbacks, but
the team recovered. You've probably experienced something similar in your own life. There are many times when
situations don't go how you planned—in the workplace,
at home, or in relationships. Sometimes we go into things
expecting success only to find out that we have a lot of
work to do to get those personal wins.

But you, too, can turn this season of your life around!

SCOOP UP THE BALL

Have you ever felt like success is right before you, but
someone else has come into the game and fumbled the

ball and put your chances of success at risk? Take a deep breath, lower your level, and scoop up the ball. You can do it. Drive forward in your life or relationships, and stretch for the first down. Many times, a personal victory comes from one defining moment in time.

Fear is often what holds us back from success. Ask yourself what negative thoughts and emotions are setting you back, and then affirm yourself in the moments you feel those fears or pressures. When you know what attitude or emotion is holding you back, call it out. Force yourself to overcome fear with positive and affirming thoughts. Wake up every day with a Harbaugh mindset—attack each day—and then repeat that same mindset throughout the rest of your day. You can do it, and each time you press forward is like gaining another clutch first down. No setback has to define you, and you can look at each setback as an opportunity to springboard to your greatest victory. Go Blue!

Is there a ball in your life that you need to scoop up? At work? At home? Or in a relationship? If so, what do you need to do to get that first down?

_____

_____

_____

_____

_____

_____

_____

_____

_____

GIVE THE ROSES WHILE YOU CAN

Del Duduit

November 20, 1976: Michigan 20, Ohio State 0

ROB LYTLE LED THE WAY as Michigan clinched its first Rose Bowl appearance in four years by thumping rival Ohio State University 20–0 and sharing the Big Ten title with the Buckeyes. The tailback from Fremont, Ohio, plowed his way through the OSU defense and rushed for 165 yards. He could not be stopped.

For Lytle, this was a typical game. Many called him one of Michigan head football coach Bo Schembechler's favorite players, although he'd had to earn this distinction.

During his freshman year in 1973, he was the eighth tailback on the Wolverines roster, but his coaches noticed his reputation as a hard-nosed running machine. They liked his driven mentality and toughness.

As a sophomore in 1974, he was the team's second-leading rusher with 802 yards on 140 carries for an average of 5.7 yards. He got the nod at fullback his junior year and was the second-leading rusher with 1,030 yards on 193 carries (average: 5.3 yards) in 12 games.

His senior year, he shifted to tailback and led Michigan to a Big Ten Conference Championship title. The Wolverines finished 10–2 and ranked number three in the Associated Press Poll. He led the team in rushing with 1,469 yards on 221 carries, scored fourteen touchdowns, received a selection to the first team All-American, and placed third in the Heisman Trophy voting.

While wearing Maize and Blue, Lytle set a school record with 3,307 yards rushing, which wasn't broken until five years later. He carried on his football career in the NFL as a Denver Bronco, receiving the forty-fifth pick overall in the 1977 draft. Over his seven-year career, he ran for 1,451 yards and scored fourteen touchdowns. He was the first player to score a touchdown in both the Rose Bowl and the Super Bowl. Lytle died in 2010 but was posthumously inducted into the College Football Hall of Fame in 2015.

Who is the Rob Lytle in your life—that person who stands out, pushes forward, and always gives it their all, no matter what? How did that person go above and beyond, and how did that benefit you?

LOOK OVER THE DEFENSE

Does someone you know deserve public accolades or recognition? Perhaps a teacher or coach meant a great deal to you, and you never thanked them. Like many people, you assumed they did not want acknowledgment or were "just doing their job." Maybe you feel like you've taken a loved one for granted and want to convey a special message to them before it's too late.

Perhaps the person you want to thank lives with you or close by, or maybe they are hundreds of miles away.

No matter how near or far, take the initiative to find someone who deserves your gratitude and show them your appreciation. Don't procrastinate any longer, or else when they're gone, you will have to live with the regret of never telling them. You've thought about it for a while, and the time for action is now.

GO FOR THE PYLON

You can show your gratitude in many ways. Take note of the person's birthday and send a card or gift. Social media is nice, but a handwritten letter adds a personal touch. You can also send a Christmas or holiday card. When you allocate a few moments of your time, it will mean a lot to the person on the receiving end. Invite them to coffee or lunch. If the person lives close to you, take them out to brunch as a sign of appreciation. If you run into them at the coffee shop, buy their drink. Realize that the little things matter.

If the person you want to show thanks to is part of your immediate family—your spouse, your children, your parents—tell them how you feel every day. When I became a father in my midtwenties, I realized just how much my parents had sacrificed for me. In return, I got into the habit of checking in on them on a regular basis. I cut the grass for my dad often, and I took my mom shopping and ran errands for her when she became older. I did this not out of guilt but out of gratitude.

Rob Lytle gave his all for Michigan fans. He played hard and sacrificed daily in workouts and practices to perform well. In the end, he was posthumously inducted into the College Football Hall of Fame, so he did not get to receive his ultimate reward for his dedication. You have the opportunity today to tell someone special what they mean to you before it's too late. Go Blue!

Is there someone who deserves your gratitude? Think of three people and act today!

_____
_____
_____
_____
_____
_____
_____
_____
_____
_____
_____
_____
_____
_____
_____
_____
_____
_____
_____
_____
_____
_____
_____
_____
_____
_____
_____

TURNING POINT

Cyle Young

October 15, 2005: Penn State at Michigan

PENNSYLVANIA STATE UNIVERSITY ROLLED INTO
Ann Arbor expecting to trounce the floundering University of Michigan Wolverines. The Nittany Lions were undefeated, and their 6–0 record was Penn State's best start
since 1999. The 3–3 Wolverines had experienced an equal
share of offensive and defensive struggles over the course
of the 2005 season. Their lone bright spot entering the
Penn State game was the fact that Michigan had dominated the last six games in the series, including a 27–24
overtime win in 2002. For whatever reason, Michigan had
become Penn State's Achilles' heel.

The Nittany Lions were intent on ending the losing
record and taking back control of the series. If Penn State's
stellar dual-threat quarterback had anything to do with it,
that was exactly what they'd do.

But the first half didn't go as expected—for either team.
The game turned into a defensive battle. With 4:34 left in
the second quarter, the score was 3–0. Michigan held a
small and unexpected lead on a Garrett Rivas field goal.

The Wolverines entered the third quarter with the new-found belief not only that they could they win but also that they held the lead and the momentum. Michigan extended their lead to 10–0 with a ten-play 72-yard drive early in the third quarter. With ten seconds left in the third, Penn State finally found the scoreboard on a Kevin Kelly 25-yard field goal.

But a well-coached team can never be counted out, and in seventeen seconds, everything changed.

Penn State quarterback Michael Robinson scored on a 4-yard run early in the fourth quarter. On the Wolverines' next play, quarterback Chad Henne fumbled the ball, and Nittany Lion cornerback Alan Zemaitis scooped the ball up and returned it for a 35-yard Penn State touchdown. A surprise 2-point conversion by Kevin Kelly gave the Nittany Lions an 18–10 lead.

Michigan would respond to the adversity well. Henne tossed a 33-yard touchdown pass to Mario Manningham, and Mike Hart's 2-point conversion tied the game at 18. The fourth quarter was becoming a game of its own.

The Wolverines forced Penn State to punt on their next drive, and after a nine-play drive, Rivas gave the Wolverines the lead with a 47-yard field goal. Two plays later, Michigan cornerback Leon Hall intercepted Robinson, and the Wolverines looked to be in control of the game once again. Michigan drove into field goal range, but instead of taking a long 51-yard field goal, Michigan punted to the Penn State 19-yard line.

With just under four minutes to go in the game, Penn State had 81 yards standing between them and victory. Robinson looked like a pro as he led his offense down the field and converted a fourth-and-seven. With no time-outs left, he capped the drive with a 4-yard touchdown run to give his team a 4-point lead. With fifty-three seconds left in the game, it looked as though Penn State would end their losing streak.

On the ensuing kickoff, Michigan's Steve Breaston returned the ball to near midfield, giving his team a chance to win the game. Henne led his team to the Penn State 10-yard line, and with one second left on the clock, the Wolverines had one final play to determine the outcome of the game.

Henne found wide receiver Mario Manningham in the middle of the end zone, and with time expiring, the Wolverines took a 27–25 lead. The victory extended Michigan's streak of wins over Penn State to seven in a row.

Though the contest was tough, the Wolverines never counted themselves out. In their minds, they knew they could defeat the Nittany Lions. It didn't matter what the media predicted. And it didn't matter what Vegas oddsmakers thought was going to happen. The resilient team persevered—they believed in themselves and in each other.

Do you believe in yourself that much? When others count you out, do you rise to the occasion? Or do you crash under the pressure?

MAKE THE FINAL PLAY

Have you ever experienced a moment in life where everything hangs on your next play? Maybe you are at one of those crossroads right now. Have faith and know that you can have success, even if you have the pressure of a crowd watching your every move. Just like Chad Henne, you can find your receiver in the back of the end zone, and you can have success.

COMPLETE THE CONVERSION

You don't have to let previous setbacks and defeats define you. The 2005 Wolverines didn't. In life, you have to make peace with your past failures. Cut yourself some slack. We all mess up and experience failure. Shake off your past failures and regain control of your life, one decision at a time. Your failures don't define you. Successful people are always defined by how they overcome setbacks and push forward to triumph. Every great quarterback has a short memory of incompletions and interceptions, you too need to have a short memory of life's hurdles and disappointments. Go Blue!

What do you need to do to make that game-winning throw in your life right now?

_____

_____

_____

_____

_____

_____

_____

_____

_____

_____

_____

_____

_____

_____

LEAVE A LEGACY

Del Duduit

October 27, 1979: Michigan 27, Indiana 21

THE GAME WAS TIED AT 21. Lee Corso's Indiana University Hoosiers had knotted the game with one minute to play in the final quarter. In 1979, there was no overtime rule, and a stalemate would have a negative impact on the University of Michigan team, which was 6–1 overall and 4–0 in conference play. The Wolverines took the ball and drove to the Indiana 45-yard line. They needed a miracle to win.

The choice was clear. There was only one option.

Wide receiver Anthony Carter boldly told quarterback Johnny Wagner that he was going to be open and to hit him with a pass downfield. Carter zigzagged down the middle and reeled in the throw near the Indiana 20-yard line. But there was more to come. He made a cutback move to his left to avoid one tackle and slipped another one at the 5-yard line before romping into the end zone with no time left on the clock.

The play gave him a Big Ten Conference record with thirty-seven touchdown catches over his career, but he will forever be immortalized in Michigan history for his stunning score as time expired to beat Indiana. People in Michigan still talk about the play today, and it is regarded as one of the best efforts ever in Maize and Blue history.

In an interview with AnnArbor.com in 2009, Carter recalled the feat thirty years later as if it happened yesterday. He said the play has meant the world to him and the fans. No matter what happens in Michigan football, no one will ever be able to take away the memory of that exciting last-second touchdown in 1979.

Anthony Carter has long been remembered for this phenomenal play. But it wasn't the only great thing he did during his time at Michigan, where Coach Bo Schembechler referred to Carter as a human torpedo. During his freshman year, he hauled in seventeen passes and converted seven of these into touchdowns, averaging an incredible 27.2 yards per catch.

The next season, as a sophomore, he was the squad's MVP. He was a three-time All-American at Michigan and came in third in voting for the Heisman Trophy his senior year. In 2001, he was elected to the College Football Hall of Fame.

How will you be remembered? Does your legacy matter to you?

LOOK OVER THE DEFENSE

Is there one act you are best noted for in life? Will your legacy be positive, or will you leave gloomy memories? Perhaps you have done some things in your past you are not proud of. Maybe a bad relationship has left you with a negative image. You are not alone. No one is perfect, and everyone makes mistakes. But you also must realize you have time to redeem yourself and start over if you have messed up in life. The clock is ticking, but there is still time to make a dazzling touchdown and leave a lasting impression.

GO FOR THE PYLON

No matter what you have done or what has happened to you, once you realize there is a better way and a path to redemption, you can have a brighter outlook on life. But in this process you must take responsibility, own up to your mistakes, and manage your missed opportunities. You can either let your regrets hold you down or use them to motivate you and learn from the experience.

Face reality and recognize that every decision has a consequence. Wrong choices may lead to a horrible situation, but you can rise above it when you acknowledge that it happened. Don't sugarcoat it or pretend it was a dream. Wake up and address the problem head-on. Set your mind right. You must make sure all the negative thoughts are out of your head. A positive mind-set is an important factor in leaving a legacy. You want to do good and make up for some of your past mistakes. It can happen, but you must be patient. Seek out the motivation you need.

Michigan fans held on to hope for the last play against Indiana. The players did, too. If the team had given up and hadn't tried, then Carter's famous play would never have happened. Go into each day with the expectation that something good is going to take place.

Carter finished his career at Michigan as a legend. He'd started out as a normal receiver with the same expectations as every other player. He worked hard at his craft and took advantage of opportunities and made the most of his career. He didn't catch every pass thrown to him and made his share of mistakes. But he had a plan and a positive outlook. When you showcase those attributes, you, too, can make a phenomenal play. Go Blue!

What can you do to make people remember you in a positive way?

_____

_____

_____

_____

_____

_____

_____

_____

_____

_____

_____

_____

_____

_____

_____

_____

_____

_____

_____

_____

_____

_____

_____

POINT-A-MINUTE

Cyle Young

October 8, 1902: Michigan Agricultural College at Michigan

THE SECOND SEASON UNDER LEGENDARY head coach Fielding Yost brought more victories and another national title to the University of Michigan, who finished the 1902 season with an 11–0 record while outscoring opponents 644–12. The Wolverines scored so fast and so often that these early teams have been labeled "Point-a-Minute" teams. In reality the 1902 team scored more than just a point a minute, but the title has a certain panache.

Michigan Agricultural College entered the game with a 1–1 record. The 1902 game was their second contest ever versus the University of Michigan. Their first meeting in 1898 had ended with a Michigan victory, 39–0.

The University of Michigan entered the second contest on the back of two overwhelming victories against Case Western Reserve University and Albion College for a combined total score of 136–6. But those victories came at a cost. Michigan had announced that star players Willie Heston and Everett Sweeley would not play in the game against Michigan Agricultural.

That fact alone had to give Michigan Agricultural a spark of hope. They may actually have stood a chance against the vaunted Michigan team.

But the rivals from East Lansing struggled in the game. They managed only three first downs and were able to hold Michigan on downs just one time. The *Detroit Free Press* noted that if Heston and Sweeley had participated, the result would have been much worse: "The opinion is quite general that if Heston and Sweeley had been in the game, the Buffalo record would have been beaten, but, as it was, Michigan was simply fagged out for running down the field for touchdowns."

Eight different Michigan players scored touchdowns. The team's leading scorer, Albert Herrnstein, completed seven touchdowns (at this time they counted for only 5 points each; a 1912 rule change increased a touchdown's value to 6 points). Kicker James Lawrence converted 19 points after touchdowns—more in one game than some kickers converted in an entire season. Outside of Michigan's 1901 victory over Buffalo 128–0, the *Michigan Alumnus* called the game "the greatest fusillade of touchdowns ever known to the football world."

Not many Michigan fans realize that this 119–0 victory was the biggest win in Michigan's storied rivalry with Michigan State University. In 1925 Michigan Agricultural College would change its name to Michigan State College of Agricultural Science and Applied Science and then in 1964 to the now recognized Michigan State University.

What has been the biggest, most successful moment in your life so far? How were you able to reach that goal or achieve that dream?

BE A GOOD SPORT

Fielding Yost had a reputation for running up the score on his opponents, but the 1902 game ended early because both teams realized it was over. The Michigan team was far ahead of Michigan Agricultural in terms of both talent and personnel. In the spirit of good sportsmanship, both coaches, Yost and Denman, agreed to call the game early with two minutes still remaining on the clock. Similarly, your success doesn't have to depreciate or denigrate others. If you are having great success in life, make sure that you aren't rubbing it in to others. Take Yost's example to heart, think about how your success affects those around you, and do not rub it in—even if you have done so in the past.

But also remember to enjoy your success and accomplishments and work hard to keep your momentum!

SCORE A POINT A MINUTE

It's okay to perform as expected. Success in life *is* allowed. When all the pieces come together, you can accomplish amazing things. All the hard work you put into your work and relationships should one day pay off, and when that day comes, you can celebrate.

If you are experiencing times of great success right now, take a moment and pat yourself on the back—you deserve it. But also remember that to maintain success at home and at work requires a consistent willingness to continue to improve as a person. Go Blue!

Are you happy with your level of success in life? Why, or why not?

TALK THE TALK, WALK THE WALK

Del Duduit

November 22, 1986: Michigan 26, Ohio State 24

THE UNIVERSITY OF MICHIGAN WOLVERINES were fresh off their first loss of the season to the University of Minnesota and headed to Columbus, Ohio, to face their archrival the Ohio State Buckeyes. Michigan still had high hopes for the season, and a win over Ohio State would mean a great deal to the team and coach Bo Schembechler.

The tone of the game had been set days ahead of the contest. A few days before the two teams met, Michigan quarterback Jim Harbaugh channeled his inner Joe Namath and went public with a prediction. "I guarantee we'll beat Ohio State this Saturday. We'll be in Pasadena on January 1. There's no doubt in my mind about that," he said.

Few athletes have gone on to back up what they say in public. Namath had been right when his New York Jets had upset the Baltimore Colts 16–7 to win Super Bowl III in 1969. In 1985, Larry Bird announced he would win the inaugural NBA 3-point shootout, and he did. And in 1963,

Muhammad Ali rhymed, "It ain't no jive, Henry Cooper will go in five." The greatest of all time was right, and he won by TKO in the fifth round.

In 1986, Harbaugh went out on a limb and had to back up his words. During the game, both sides exhibited fantastic performances. Ohio State's running back Vince Workman rushed for 126 yards on twenty-one carries, while quarterback Jim Karsatos was fifteen of twenty-seven for 188 yards and two touchdowns. Receiver Cris Carter hauled in seven passes for 75 yards and two touchdowns for the Bucks.

For the Maize and Blue, Jamie Morries slashed through the Buckeye defense for 210 yards on twenty-nine carries and two TDs. Then there was Harbaugh, who finished the game nineteen of twenty-nine in the air for 261 yards and the win. His offense accumulated a whopping 529 yards.

But the win was not a gimme by any means. In fact, Ohio State held a 7–3 lead in the first quarter. Karsatos connected with Carter on a 4-yard TD. The Buckeyes increased their advantage 14–3 when Workman galloped 43 yards for the score.

Schembechler made adjustments at the half, and his Wolverines took control of the final two periods. Harbaugh managed scoring drives of 85, 83, and 76 yards. With 1:06 to play in the game, Michigan had a 26–24 lead. Ohio State had the ball on the Michigan 28 and faced a fourth down. Coach Earl Bruce opted to attempt a field goal to try to win the game. But Ohio State kicker Matt Franz missed the kick, and Michigan won the epic battle. Harbaugh had been right on both counts: His Wolverines beat Ohio State and went to Pasadena in the Rose Bowl.

What guarantees in life have you made? Have you promised to spend more time with your children or that special person in your life? Have you met your commitments?

DESIGN YOUR PLAY

Maybe you have fantastic intentions, but life's events have altered your plans. Maybe you told your son or daughter you would be at their game or recital and stayed late for work instead. Perhaps you promised to take your spouse to dinner and simply forgot. Life happens. That is no excuse, but it can be a reality.

EXECUTE YOUR GAME PLAN

You made plans for that special weekend with your partner or talked about a once-in-a-lifetime vacation or pledged to get the honey-do list finished—but time got away from you. The key to success is to follow through on your obligations as soon as possible. Don't offer lip service to sound good, because that leads only to disappointment. Make a realistic vow, and back it up.

When you put off doing what you said you would do, it creates stress and anxiety. If a problem comes up, don't make an excuse but communicate on a regular basis. Be clear about expectations, and always be honest. If you cannot meet your obligation, be up front and take responsibility. Be careful not to make too many promises. Harbaugh guaranteed only one victory, and he came through. Don't go out on a limb too many times, because that limb will eventually break off. Commit yourself only when you are sure you can honor your word.

In the end, you must come through. No excuses. Have the mind-set to underpromise and overdeliver because that will score you big points and send you to the family Rose Bowl. Your kids want time with you, too, so come through for the ones who count the most. The after-work emails can wait, and your golfing buddies will understand. Family and commitments take priority. Go Blue!

What obligations mean the most to you? How do you ensure you fulfill them?

_____

_____

_____

_____

_____

_____

_____

_____

_____

_____

_____

_____

_____

_____

_____

_____

_____

_____

_____

_____

_____

_____

THROW THE BALL TO ME

Cyle Young

October 27, 1979: Indiana at Michigan

HOMECOMING WEEKEND 1979, THE 5–1 University of Michigan Wolverines met Lee Corso's 5–2 Indiana University Hoosiers on the field in Michigan Stadium. Even in those days, Indiana wasn't a powerhouse of college football. But in 1979 the Hoosiers pulled together their best season under Corso. They'd go on to finish the season ranked sixteenth in the country, propelled by a huge victory over undefeated Brigham Young University in the Holiday Bowl.

But midway through the season, the Michigan faithful weren't too concerned over a serious challenge from Indiana. Even through three-quarters of the football game, Michigan seemed to be firmly in control. The Wolverines carried a 21–7 lead over into the fourth quarter, and the game seemed to be well in hand.

However, Indiana wasn't going to just lie down and let the Wolverines have another easy victory. Quarterback Tim Clifford led his team down the field, and the Hoosiers brought the game to within 7 points. The Indiana defense toughened during the fourth, and they held Michigan to a series of stalled drives.

Despite the fourth-quarter offensive difficulties, the Wolverines still seemed in control of the game and looked like they'd leave Michigan Stadium with a win—until Indiana scored with less than a minute to go in the game, bringing the score to 21–21. Leaving Ann Arbor with a tie would be considered a massive accomplishment for the Indiana team and a significant letdown for Michigan, whose coach, Bo Schembechler, wouldn't be happy.

The Wolverine offense, led by quarterback John Wangler and wide receiver Anthony Carter, took control of the ball on their own 22 with fifty-one seconds left on the clock. They needed to at least get the team into field goal range. Fifty yards in fifty seconds would give them an opportunity to kick for the win.

Wangler drove the team down the field, and the Wolverines crossed midfield. With six seconds left in the game, running back Lawrence Reid pitched the ball out of bounds at the Indiana 45-yard line. The strategy worked, and the clock stopped (it is no longer a legal maneuver today).

Schembechler didn't believe they could make the 52-yard field goal, so they called a pass. In the huddle, Wangler called the play, an in-route. Carter looked him straight in the eyes and said, "Wangs, you throw the ball to me."

With six seconds left, Wangler dropped back. Carter split the defenders and caught a perfectly thrown pass from Wangler on the 20-yard line. An Indiana defender attempted to trip him at the 18, but off-balance Carter charged through it. Another defender made a diving attempt at his feet at the 5-yard line, but Carter plunged forward, stepping through the ill-fated tackle, and burst through the goal line.

The stadium erupted. The Wolverines charged the field, and fans poured over the stadium walls. Coach Schembechler bounded for joy, and famed announcer Bob Ufer screamed in exaltation. Victory was secured.

Anthony Carter had known he could win the game. He had confidence in his own ability and in his team. When the game is on the line, you want the ball in your best player's hands, and without a doubt, Carter was the best player to secure a chance at victory for the 1979 Wolverines. Because of Carter's confidence, the Wolverines won the game on one of the greatest single plays in the history of Michigan football.

Do you have that kind of confidence at work or at home? When the game is on the line, do you want the ball?

PUSH IT OVER THE GOAL LINE

You, too, can have confidence in yourself and your team—your family, coworkers, friends. That kind of confidence comes from within. It's a knowledge that you *can* do it. The chances that Michigan could win the game on a 45-yard touchdown pass with six seconds to go were very small, but they did it—and you can, too. You just have to have confidence and believe in yourself.

Many times, that's all it takes in life. You just have to believe that the outcome you want is achievable and attainable. And then you have to put the effort in to achieve that desired outcome. It is that simple—so start believing in you.

SCORE A TOUCHDOWN

Many people never achieve their goals because they don't plan for success. You can create your own success by understanding why your goal is important to you. You have to have a reason you want to accomplish something. Don't let other people in your life set your goals. It's okay to share someone else's goal, but make it your own too. Give it your whole heart. When you are setting your own goals, aim high. But don't forget to set smaller objectives along the way. Celebrate each little success on your way to achieving your biggest goal, and then once you reach it, celebrate some more and set a higher target. Go Blue!

Is there an area of your life where you are struggling to have confidence in yourself? Do you believe that you can accomplish great things? Why, or why not? What changes do you need to make today to see different outcomes?

_____

_____

_____

_____

_____

_____

_____

_____

_____

_____

_____

_____

_____

_____

_____

COME OFF THE BENCH AND MAKE AN IMPACT

Del Duduit

November 23, 1996: Michigan 13, Ohio State 9

MICHIGAN ROLLED INTO COLUMBUS, OHIO, a 17-point underdog to number-two-ranked Ohio State. The Buckeyes were undefeated and had hopes of a national championship and a trip to the Rose Bowl on their minds.

The Wolverines set a defensive tone early on, even though they did not score in the first half. Ohio State drove the ball inside the red zone three times but had to settle for three field goals. Offensively Michigan struggled, and Brian Griese was put in at quarterback at the half to try to boost the offense.

He had an immediate impact. On the second play in the third quarter, he connected on a slant pass to Tai Streets for a score to cut into the Buckeye lead. Now the Michigan ground game finally came to life. The Wolverines rushed for 49 yards in the next drive, which ended with a field goal and a 10–9 lead.

The Buckeyes had opportunities but could not capital-ize on chances to score. Michigan, on the other hand, was determined to put the ball in the end zone and win the game. A twelve-play drive that marched 67 yards and ate up five minutes of the clock culminated with a 39-yard field goal and a 13–9 lead.

Now the defense had to rise to the occasion. Marcus Ray made sure that happened when he picked off a pass for the Wolverines to secure the win, upset the Buckeyes, and end Ohio State's dreams of a national championship. There was no better feeling in the world than ruining the aspirations of the Scarlet and Gray.

In the second half alone, Michigan outgained the Buck-eyes 237 yards to 84. Griese's courage and determination provided a spark to the struggling Michigan offense and inspired the defense to hold strong.

What can you do to motivate others? How do your actions affect the other players on your team?

LOOK OVER THE DEFENSE

Perhaps you are on the bench and watching the game of life go by. You are consumed with your own agenda and have not given much attention to your team. You want them to win, and you put in your time at practice with the hope of seeing the field one day. You go to work and come home and live a good life, but you want more. You have a desire to contribute to a big win. But how? All you need is one chance to let everyone know what you can do on the field.

Then suddenly, you get the call. You are thrust into the game. Are you ready? What will you do to provide a spark in your life and to those around you?

GO FOR THE PYLON

You don't have to make a dramatic interception or score a last-second touchdown to be considered a winner. You can have an impact on someone's life with simple acts of kindness. Consider a way to donate your time. Instead of spending a Saturday on the golf course or at the lake, stop in and give your time at a homeless shelter. Volunteer at a soup kitchen or go through your closet and find good clothes to take to the Salvation Army. Time is your most valued commodity. When you give it, you will come off the bench and have an impact.

Make family your highest priority. If you have children, try never to put anything in front of their needs. There are times when work must come first, but that should be a rare occasion. If your son has a game in the evening, you need to try to be there. When your daughter has a dance class, make the effort to support her. Your family needs your attention more than your boss. Take a Sunday afternoon and pamper your spouse. When you put your family first, the rest falls into place.

Surprise someone. Pay for a person's meal in the line behind you at a restaurant or buy some flowers for a person in the hospital you may not know. Rake the leaves for your neighbor or help a widow with her yard work. Give to worthy causes. My wife and I pick four charities and contribute to them each year. There are many organizations out there that need financial support; do research, find causes you have a personal interest in, and make regular contributions to them. You can give your money, your time, or both.

Play by the rules and work hard. Give your employer an honest day's work. When you do this, you are holding yourself accountable and showing those around you that integrity is still alive. You may not like your job, but honor your commitment and be an example.

Brian Griese put in his time on the practice field and was ready when called. You need to do the little things in life and prepare for your moment of truth. Adopt a solid routine and make an impact every day in your life. Go Blue!

Can you think of three worthy causes to which you can contribute your time or money? Is there a person in your life you could reach out and lend a hand to?

_____

_____

_____

_____

_____

_____

_____

_____

_____

_____

_____

_____

_____

_____

_____

_____

_____

_____

_____

THE POSE

Cyle Young

November 23, 1991: Ohio State at Michigan

THE 1991 GAME BETWEEN OHIO State and the University of Michigan wasn't exceptional. In history it would hardly be a blip on the radar of greatest sports moments . . . if it weren't for legendary Heisman Trophy winner Desmond Howard.

Michigan controlled the entire game, which they would easily win 31–3. The Buckeyes came into the game fresh after it was announced that their head coach, John Copper, had received a three-year extension to his contract. But that news was the only bright spot for Ohio State's team.

A massive crowd of 106,156 fans piled into Michigan Stadium to watch the Wolverines decimate their hated rival from Ohio. Michigan scored quickly on a fake field goal to give them a 7–0 lead. The Buckeyes responded with a long drive to the Wolverine 28, but a corresponding field goal fell short of the post.

Michigan running back Ricky Powers fumbled away the ball on the Wolverines' next possession, and the

Buckeyes capitalized on the turnover with a field goal to bring the game to 7–3. That's the closest the score got. On the ensuing drive, the Wolverines intercepted the Buckeyes and, one drive later, sent the game out of reach.

A couple of series later, magic would happen. A play that continues to live in infamy, even to this day. Ohio State's punter kicked the ball to the Wolverine 7-yard line. Desmond Howard positioned himself to receive the punt. When the ball landed in his arms, Howard shot forward like a rocket. He blasted past five Buckeye defenders, splitting through the middle of the Ohio State kick coverage before sprinting down the left sideline. By the time he reached the Ohio State 20-yard line, Howard was 5 yards ahead of his closest defender. No one could catch him.

Howard pumped his arm into the sky and traversed halfway across the end zone before pausing to strike the famous one-leg-raised Heisman pose. Howard's season had been one for the record books. He punctuated the game on the biggest stage in the country, against the team's biggest rival, with a statement for the Heisman selection committee: he was the best football player in the country.

And the committee agreed. A couple of weeks later, Howard became Michigan's second Heisman trophy winner. But back on November 23, 1991, he wasn't done making statements. In the third quarter he caught a 50-yard pass, and in the fourth quarter he caught a 42-yard strike in double coverage.

The game solidified Howard's legend and created a Heisman craze. Since 1991, every football player who strikes the Heisman pose does it just like Desmond

Howard did—even though the pose is incorrect. The actual Heisman statue has two feet on the ground.

The 1991 game could have just been another day at the office for Desmond Howard—but it wasn't. He turned what could have been a boring contest into a life-changing event. Howard didn't settle for mediocrity; he went out and changed the world, one play at a time.

What's your play when the game depends on you? Can you pick up the ball and run with it to bring your team to victory?

CARRY THE BALL

You can change your world, too. Don't let yourself be stuck in mediocrity. And don't let each day be as boring as the rest. Find unique ways to create your own success each day. Set achievable goals for yourself: maybe you want to try to win employee of the month at work, become the top sales leader in your industry, or receive a significant performance bonus. You can do it. All it takes is an attitude of excellence and a mind focused on achieving your intended goal.

What's your plan? What can you do today in order to reach the goals you set for yourself?

WIN YOUR HEISMAN

What are your goals in life? At work and at home? Maybe you want to get a new position or a raise. Or maybe you'd like to take time for a vacation with your family. List below what you want to work toward in your personal life and at work, and then list three steps to help you achieve your goal and win your personal Heisman. Go Blue!

Personal Goal: _____

1. _____
2. _____
3. _____

Work Goal: _____

1. _____
2. _____
3. _____

SUMMER WORKOUTS

DON'T TAKE LIFE
FOR GRANTED

Del Duduit

September 1, 2007: Appalachian State 34, Michigan 32

NO ONE EXPECTED THIS.

Michigan fans had high hopes for this squad. The Wolverines were ranked number five in the nation, and prognosticators pinned them as a favorite to win the Big Ten Conference Championship. There were also some experts who felt the Maize and Blue could even contend for the national title. This was supposed to be their year.

The Appalachian State Mountaineers were ranked number one in the Sports Network Football Championship Subdivision and were favored to win a third straight title. But they still were not considered a threat to contend with Michigan, let alone beat them. All predictions had the Wolverines as heavy favorites, and bookies in Las Vegas did not give a betting line.

The game was the first one broadcast on the Big Ten Network. Appy State jumped out to a 28–17 lead by the break. The Big House fans were stunned. Could this happen? What was going on?

Michigan started a drive in the fourth quarter to try to come back to reality and get into the game. The Wolverines clawed their way back into contention. Running back Mike Hart galloped 54 yards for the touchdown, and they had a 32–31 lead with just under five minutes to play in the game.

Michigan later attempted a field goal, but it was blocked, and the Mountaineers received the ball with 1:37 to play. Then, with twenty-six seconds remaining, Appy State nailed a field goal and went ahead 34–32.

With little time left on the clock, Michigan quarterback Chad Henne connected with Mario Manningham for a 46-yard pass and put the Wolverines in position for a game-winning 37-yard field goal.

But lightning struck twice as the Mountaineers blocked the kick again and secured the win. The game was touted as one of the biggest upsets in Michigan history, as well as in college sports. Commentators were speechless, as was the Michigan fanbase. Dan Wetzel of Yahoo! Sports wrote after the contest:

> This game was supposed to be the prime example of what had gone wrong in money hungry college football. The powers that be had expanded the season a couple years back, adding an extra game so big schools could bring in cream-puff opponents while collecting millions in revenue. Michigan had never played a I-AA opponent in its history. Now we know why, the Wolverines were ducking them. Instead of an easy tune-up for Michigan, Appalachian State leaves with its most profound victory ever and a check for $400,000 that was supposed to be their pay for getting punished.

Many teams "pad their schedule" early in the season to get off to a good start, while other squads take advantage of opportunities to play on the big stage.

Did Michigan take this game for granted? Or did Appalachian State play the game of its life? Maybe both. All that mattered was the outcome. Michigan lost a game it should have won.

LOOK OVER THE DEFENSE

Have you ever found yourself in a similar situation? Perhaps you feel you are entitled to some of the better things in life. Maybe you are in line for a job promotion or that deal of a lifetime on a truck you've had your eye on for a while. Or you might think you have a relationship in the bag and that the other person is lucky to have you. Then, just when you think it's all going to fall into place, your field goal is blocked, and you lose the game.

Were you ever so sure you were going to win, but you ended up losing? What could you have done differently to ensure a better outcome?

GO FOR THE PYLON

Don't wait for the kick to be blocked. Take action now to put yourself in position to win the contest. It's easy to become comfortable in situations where you think you've got it made, but watch out for the yellow flags. To be sure you don't get called for a penalty, try a couple of techniques.

1. Show gratitude: Appreciate what you have, and strive to gain relationships you long for in the future. Never let one or two minor flaws stand in the way of something wonderful. After all, you are not perfect, and your employer, your spouse, or someone you are dating can overlook that, so you should, too. Instead, appreciate

their uniqueness and celebrate them for who they are, not what you want them to be.

2. Go out of your own way: Do something little for them that you may consider insignificant. Don't suck up, but show appreciation with a small act of kindness. A simple birthday card or gift card to their favorite restaurant is always welcome. Find out their favorite author and buy a book for them. Little acts of kindness and thoughtfulness can score points and lead to a big win.

When you become complacent, you can put yourself at risk for a tremendous upset. Stay focused on your game plan, and perform the basic plays. Recognize your weakness and make sure your kick is never blocked. Don't take anyone or any circumstance for granted. Go Blue!

List three of your weaknesses and plans to overcome them.

_____
_____
_____
_____
_____
_____
_____
_____
_____
_____
_____
_____
_____
_____
_____
_____
_____

WEEK 14

—w—

CIGAR IN HAND

Cyle Young

January 1, 1981: University of Washington vs. Michigan

WITH A CAREER COACHING RECORD of 234 wins, 65 losses, and 8 ties, University of Michigan head coach Bo Schembechler was obviously successful. He is not just one of the greatest University of Michigan coaches of all time; he is one of the greatest college football coaches of all time.

But leading up to the 1981 Rose Bowl against the University of Washington, Schembechler was a loser because up until that point in his tenure, he had failed to win any of the seven bowl games Michigan had been in. He was the butt of many jokes; the media had a lot of fun poking jabs at Schembechler's terrible bowl record. The day before the Rose Bowl, a United Press International (UPI) story asked, "Why doesn't Bo Schembechler eat cereal for breakfast? He's afraid he'd lose the bowl." A Garnett reporter even noted that Michigan's new theme song wasn't "The Victors" but "Taps."

On January 1, 1981, Schembechler knew the pressure was on. Not only did his team need a Rose Bowl win, but he personally needed the win.

Michigan entered the game against Washington as the favorite. Their staunch defense, anchored by co-captain Andy Cannavino, had stifled teams all season long and hadn't allowed an opponent to score a touchdown in the last eighteen quarters of the season. The intimidating Michigan offensive line was just as impressive and featured four future NFL players, including All-American center George Lilja. And, of course, the legendary Michigan receiver Anthony Carter always gave the team a chance to win any game.

Because of the media chatter leading up to the game against Washington, even the players knew they needed to get a win for their coach. Lilja commented a few days before the game, "We want to win for our coach as much as for ourselves."

In front of a crowd of almost 105,000 fans, Michigan held the Washington offense scoreless in the first quarter. In the second quarter, the Huskies scored their only points of the game on two Chuck Nelson field goals. The staunch Michigan defense extended their streak of quarters during which an opponent did not score a touchdown to twenty-two.

Michigan running back Butch Woolfolk ran roughshod all over the Huskie defense. He finished the game with an impressive 182 yards on twenty-six carries and propelled the Wolverines to an easy Rose Bowl victory. Woolfolk's impressive individual performance would garner him the game's MVP award.

When the clock struck zero, Michigan players hoisted their coach on their shoulders and strutted him onto the field. Coach Schembechler raised his arms in victory— he'd finally achieved a bowl win. The jinx had been broken. Schembechler couldn't have been more excited, and at the postgame press conference he beamed, "I stood here five times before a loser. Now I'm smoking a cigar and smiling. . . . Right now, I'm on top of the world. I feel great about everything."

We can learn from Schembechler's example. He didn't give up—even after seven straight bowl losses. With all the media stories and jokes, Coach Schembechler could have ended his career early, but he was resilient. He knew that he would eventually win those games. Starting in 1981, Schembechler would go on to win five of the next ten bowl appearances—a much better result than his 0–7 start.

How do you react when it seems your losing streak will never end? Do you give up and admit defeat, or do you push forward, aiming for that elusive win?

FASTEN YOUR CHINSTRAP

Have you ever experienced a string of failures? We all do at some point or another. Those failures may not be as significant as losing seven straight bowl games, but it still stings every time. However, you don't have to let a series of setbacks ruin your outlook on life. Coach Schembechler never did. Just keep trying. Keep pushing forward, and eventually success *will* come.

BREAK THE STREAK

Have you ever faced a losing streak of your own? You can overcome any losing streak by focusing on the goal and not your emotions. People can get so wrapped up in the feeling of a loss that they lose sight of the overall goal. Every path to victory has setbacks. Life can be full of difficult journeys. You may experience situations like repeated health struggles, relationship issues, financial shortcomings, or any number of other setbacks. But in most situations you can overcome the setback with a concerted effort, a consistent strategy, and a positive attitude.

Start seeing repeated failures as repeated opportunities for even greater success. You are defined only by what you want to be defined by. Failure doesn't ever have to define you. Let your success or your eventual success be the definition of your character and persistence. Go Blue!

What can you do today that will break your losing streak and push you toward a win?

_____
_____
_____
_____
_____
_____
_____
_____
_____
_____
_____
_____
_____
_____
_____
_____
_____
_____
_____

WHAT'S IN YOUR JUG?

Del Duduit

October 31, 1903: Michigan 6, Minnesota 6

THE RIVALRY BETWEEN UNIVERSITY OF Michigan
and University of Minnesota goes back to 1892, when the
Golden Gophers knocked off the Wolverines 14–6. Since
1903, every time these two teams play each other, the winning team is awarded an earthenware pot called the Little
Brown Jug; their matchup is the oldest trophy game in
FBS (NCAA Division 1 Football Bowl Subdivision, for-
merly known as Division 1-A) college football to this day.
It is revered and an honor to win.

The Wolverines have dominated the Little Brown Jug
since the tradition started. But it was a different story in
1903.

The team was 28–0 under Yost's direction, and Minnesota had slowly put together a competitive squad, eager
to end that streak. Excitement mounted as the game drew
near. The two Big Ten teams met each other with high
hopes and about twenty thousand fans in attendance.
The high-powered Wolverine offense was slowed down
to only one touchdown. Meanwhile, the Gophers did

not manage to score until they tied it up 6–6 with about 2 minutes left in the game.

After Minnesota scored, thousands of their fans rushed the field. Faced with the combination of the crowd on the field and a looming storm, officials called the game, and a tie was declared. The Wolverines walked off the field and went home.

According to historical records, before the game, the Michigan team's student manager, Thomas Roberts, had been told to buy something to carry water in for the players, out of concern that Minnesota fans might contaminate the water. Roberts had bought a blue five-gallon jug from a local store. When the Wolverines departed the stadium on October 31, 1903, they left the jug behind. A custodian found the jug and took it to the Minnesota athletic director, L. J. Cooke, the next day. Cooke proceeded to paint the jug brown, covering up the blue, and added "Michigan 6, Minnesota 6" on the side. The Golden Gophers' score was painted much larger than Michigan's. Thus the tradition of the Little Brown Jug was born.

The next time the teams met in 1909, both schools liked the idea of playing for the jug as a traveling trophy. Michigan won it in 1909 and 1910. The two teams did not meet again until 1919, after the Wolverines rejoined the Big Ten Conference. Minnesota won the jug that year.

Fast-forward to the 2003 game at the Metrodome in Minneapolis. It was highly anticipated because it marked the one hundredth anniversary of the rivalry. The Golden Gophers were ranked number seventeen while Michigan ranked twentieth. Both teams bantered back and forth about who was going to win the Little Brown Jug, and radio shows and newspapers highlighted the event.

The Wolverines took home the jug with a 38–35 win, and they have dominated the matchup ever since. But every time the two teams meet, they have something to play for. Although it's not a national championship, each contest holds meaning. Pride is at stake, and bragging rights abound.

What do you play for? What meaning does your life have?

HOLD UP YOUR TROPHY

Have you figured out what purpose your life holds? Have your dreams been altered or your plans changed from what you originally envisioned? Has something happened in your life that has caused you to put your dreams on hold? You are not alone. This is life. You must be willing to adapt and change to your surroundings. But this does not mean you should quit or give up. There may be something else in store for you—perhaps your own Little Brown Jug.

PAINT YOUR WINS

Your childhood dreams might still happen. But you cannot let a tie game get you down. You might suffer an upset or a loss, and how you deal with it will determine your character. Celebrate each win, and learn from a loss. Once you accept defeat, you will be able to adjust and strive to win the next game. Hold strong to your values and work ethic, and imagine what magnificent things could happen in the future.

Be around people who make you smile and challenge you to pursue your dreams. Follow your heart, and push yourself to win. Be open to change, and take pleasure in the simple things in life. Hold tight to memories, and smile along the way. Happiness and success are within your grasp.

Understand what is best for you and your family. Put your priorities in order, and focus on what really matters in life. Be patient and deal with circumstances that may come your way. Life will throw some penalties at you along the way. Don't view them as setbacks but rather as opportunities to make the big play. When you do this, you will find your purpose and drink victory from your Little Brown Jug. Go Blue!

What three things mean the most to you?

_____
_____
_____
_____
_____
_____
_____
_____
_____
_____
_____
_____
_____
_____
_____
_____
_____
_____
_____
_____

CLIMBING EVEREST

Cyle Young

January 1, 1998: Washington State vs. Michigan

THE UNIVERSITY OF MICHIGAN ENTERED the eighty-fourth Rose Bowl game after going through the season undefeated. Behind the stellar play of Heisman Trophy winner Charles Woodson, quarterback Brian Griese, and All-American defensive lineman Glen Steele, Michigan had vaulted to the top of the college football rankings. In coach Lloyd Carr's third season, the Wolverines had one final game left standing between them and the national championship.

At the start of the season, Michigan was ranked number seventeen. No football analysts would have chosen them as the eventual national champion—but the 125 football players sweating and bleeding together in Schembechler Hall's practice facilities did. They knew it would be a season for the ages.

At the beginning of the season, Coach Carr revealed a giant Mount Everest mural on the wall of the team's meeting room. The Rose Bowl and the national championship rested at the summit, and the season's opponents were interspersed from the bottom to the top. With each victory, the Wolverines would climb closer to the title.

In addition, during summer practice, Coach Carr had invited Michigan native Lou Kasischke to speak to the football team about his ascent of Mt. Everest in 1996 and the tragedy surrounding it. The journey had been documented in the *New York Times* best-selling book *Into Thin Air*. The story would become the perfect metaphor for Michigan's championship season. Carr presented each player with an ice-climbing pickaxe that had been painted maize and blue. The pickaxes would hang from the ceiling all season long as a constant reminder of their perilous journey to the national championship. After eleven games and eleven wins, the summit of Everest was in sight. All that stood in the way was the Washington State Cougars.

The Rose Bowl game started with a first quarter touchdown pass by Washington State quarterback Ryan Leaf. Kevin McKenzie's 15-yard reception gave the Cougars an early lead. Michigan responded with a score of their own eleven minutes later. After the two adversaries traded punts, Wolverine quarterback Brian Griese hit receiver Tai Streets in stride for a 53-yard touchdown. Both teams would carry the tie into halftime.

On its first possession of the second half, Leaf drove his team 99 yards to take the lead. The Cougars capped the drive with a 14-yard reverse for a touchdown. Washington State wasn't just going to lie down and let the Wolverines have the championship. They were going to make them earn it.

Michigan blocked the extra point. Needing a score to retake the lead, they peeled off a series of runs with running back Chris Howard, which perfectly set up a 58-yard play-action touchdown pass from Griese to Streets. Michigan converted the extra point and retook the lead.

Washington State was held to a punt on the next drive, and Michigan once again charged down the field, capping a 77-yard drive early in the fourth quarter with a play-action touchdown pass to tight end Jerame Tuman. Michigan secured a 21–13 lead.

But Leaf was far from finished. He drove his Cougars down the field after converting a third-and-eighteen on his own 12-yard line. Washington State would settle for a field goal, bringing them within a touchdown of retaking the lead. Michigan ran out the clock on the next drive, leaving Leaf only sixteen seconds to travel 93 yards for the win.

But the Cougars were resilient, and after a couple well-planned plays and a Wolverine penalty, Washington State had two seconds left on the Michigan 26-yard line. They were within striking distance of the goal line. But as Leaf tried to spike the ball to stop the clock, time expired.

The Michigan Wolverines charged the field. They'd done it—they'd climbed those last few steps up the summit of Mt. Everest. For the first time since 1948, Michigan Wolverines were the national champions. Their number one ranking at the end of the season was a surprise to many, but the Wolverines knew their value. They understood their skill and worth.

When your own Mt. Everest stands before you, how do you react? Are you up to the challenge of scaling the mountain and achieving your goals?

CHOOSE THE RIGHT TEAM

Don't ever let anyone count you out. You can achieve great things in life if you believe in yourself. The Michigan football team was united in their belief that they were the greatest team in the country, and they supported and encouraged each other every step of the way. Make sure you surround yourself with people who believe in you and will always be there to help you climb every mountain that stands before you.

REACH THE SUMMIT

Do you have a personal Everest? A workplace Everest? A relationship Everest? Or maybe a better question is, should you create an Everest mind-set, just like the 1997 Wolverines? You can summit the Everests in your own life—you just have to keep taking one step at a time.

To climb your own Mt. Everest you must first believe yourself. Next, you need to visualize what you want before writing it down. You have to commit to the goal, climbing your mountain is no easy task. You'll need to stay focused and develop a plan of action that includes accountability. Tell someone else your goal and give them permission to keep you accountable to accomplish it. Once you begin, keep going despite any hardship until you reach your target.

Go Blue!

What's the Everest that you need to climb? What steps will you take to reach the summit?

_____

_____

_____

_____

_____

_____

WEEK 17

—∿—

MAKE A GREAT FIRST IMPRESSION

Del Duduit

August 27, 1995: Michigan 18, Virginia 17

WHAT A FIRST GAME FOR Lloyd Carr to coach at the University of Michigan.

Michigan entered the game ranked number fourteen and started a freshman for the first time under center. Early on, Virginia, ranked number fifteen, held a commanding 17–0 lead. Everything was going right for the Cavaliers. But the Maize and Blue rallied and scored 18 unanswered points on their final three possessions, including a determined final drive.

Michigan was down 17–12 with 2:35 to play in the game and had the ball on its own 20. The end zone was a long way away. With time ticking away, quarterback Scott Dreisbach orchestrated a sixteen-play drive that included a heroic first-down dive by the freshman on the Virginia 15-yard line with twelve ticks left on the clock. Things looked bleak after three straight incomplete passes. There were four seconds left, and it was fourth down. Nerves in the stadium were at an all-time high.

The quarterback dropped back and could not find his first target, which was Amani Toomer. He scanned and spotted Mercury Hayes open in the back corner and lifted the ball in the air. Hayes pulled in the final 15-yard pass between two defenders, barely keeping one foot in the end zone, to give Michigan an 18–17 win as time ran out. It was one of the greatest comebacks in Michigan's storied history.

What a debut as coach for Carr, who had taken over for Gary Moeller. Dreisbach enjoyed a record day, too. He threw for 372 yards and completed twenty-seven of fifty-two attempts, with two touchdowns and two picks. But in the final quarter, he was spot-on target. He connected on twelve of twenty-four passes for 236 yards.

What kind of first impression do you want to make? You have opportunities every day to set the tone. Whether at work or at home, someone may meet you for the first time. Your initial words and actions matter.

COME OUT OF THE TUNNEL

Maybe it's your first day at school or on the job. Perhaps you are meeting someone on a blind date. Be the real you, and don't put on a show or give the wrong indications. When things go well and you hit it off, that can have great potential for a good future relationship.

TOUCH THE BLOCK M

You are scheduled for an interview for the job of a lifetime, or maybe a blind date has been set up for you. No matter what the case may be, the thoughts people have of you within the first few minutes can establish a tone for the meeting and even for a lifetime. Smile and be pleasant. Be confident when you introduce yourself, and maintain eye contact. Don't talk too much, but when you do, be clear and direct. Resist the temptation to fill the air just to talk. Listen, pay attention, and try to find some common ground. Body language speaks volumes, so don't slouch or watch the clock. Make the person feel comfortable to be with you, and display a sense of humor.

Mercury Hayes and Scott Dreisbach helped Lloyd Carr make a fabulous first impression on Michigan fans. It was a great comeback and a wonderful day in Ann Arbor. Make sure you are prepared for that first meeting that could change your life forever. Go Blue!

How will you prepare to make a first impression?

_____

_____

_____

_____

_____

_____

_____

_____

_____

_____

_____

_____

_____

_____

_____

_____

_____

TEN-YEAR WAR

Cyle Young

November 22, 1969: Ohio State at Michigan

THE 1969 CONTEST AGAINST OHIO State University started the Ten-Year War. During the next ten years, ten Ohio State or University of Michigan teams would enter the final game of the regular season undefeated, and six teams would enter the game with only one loss. For the years between 1969 and 1978, not only was the Big Ten conference title on the line in this rivalry game, but national championship connotations surrounded almost every matchup.

Ohio State coach Woody Hayes and Michigan coach Bo Schembechler were anything but strangers to each other. Hayes had coached Schembechler at Miami University of Ohio and then mentored Schembechler would when Schembechler served as a graduate assistant and later assistant coach at Ohio State. The two coaches would remain lifelong friends, but their friendship never dimmed their desire to beat their hated rivals. In Coach Schembechler's first season as head coach of the

Wolverines, he had the difficult task of trying to defeat the juggernaut Buckeyes. But he knew that was what it would take to change the culture at Michigan. From the moment Schembechler had been hired he'd had one simple goal: beat Ohio State.

The 1969 Buckeyes had crafted one of college football's most impressive seasons. In eight games, the closest margin of victory was an astounding 27 points. Every game had been a blowout. And even more intimidating for the Wolverines, Ohio State had never trailed at any point during the season. The Buckeyes came to the game on the back of a twenty-two-game winning streak and entered Michigan Stadium in front of 103,588 fans as the number one team in the country. Ohio State was coming off a national championship as well, and a victory at Michigan would guarantee a repeat. As 17-point favorites, it seemed like they would make quick work of the Wolverines. Ohio State had everything to lose, and the 7–2 Wolverines had everything to gain.

On the opening drive of the game, Ohio State made it all the way to the Wolverines' 2-yard line. The Michigan defense held on a fourth and goal to stop the drive. But the Wolverine offense failed to get a first down, and Ohio State quickly converted the ensuing drive to 6 points after missing the extra point.

An excellent kickoff return by Michigan's Glenn Doughty would give the Wolverines a short field. A few plays and 56 yards later, Michigan would score 7 points to become the first team all season to get a lead on the behemoth Buckeyes.

Ohio State responded with a touchdown drive to regain the lead, but after failing to convert a 2-point attempt, their lead was only 12–7. The confident Buckeyes seemed to struggle against the Wolverines.

Michigan responded with another touchdown, giving running back Garvie Craw his second touchdown of the game and putting the team in the lead, 14–7. With all the momentum, Michigan defense held Ohio State to a three-and-out on their next possession. Michigan's Barry Pierson received the Buckeyes' punt and returned it all the way to the Ohio state 3-yard line.

Michigan Stadium erupted into pandemonium. Two plays later the Wolverines scored once again, escalating the lead to 9 points. The Buckeyes drove down the field to respond, but their attempt stalled on the Michigan 36. Schembechler's team scored another touchdown on the next drive, but it was called back on a penalty. They instead settled for a Tim Killian field goal, and the game went to halftime with a score of 24–12.

Ohio State trailed at halftime for the first time in just over two years. Neither team scored in the second half, and Ohio State recorded four more turnovers, bringing their total for the game to seven. Michigan's first half would be more than enough to secure the huge upset and decimate Ohio State's chance at a repeat national championship.

Just like the 1969 Wolverines, no matter how the odds are stacked against you, you can still find great success. Any team can be beaten on any given day, and you can be successful on any given day as well. The Michigan players believed they could defeat the mighty Buckeye team, and that belief carried them on to a legendary victory.

Believe in yourself even when others don't, and you will be able to accomplish great things.

RUN WITH THE BALL

Winners share common characteristics. They persevere through trials and are committed to hard work. They often exhibit humility and have high levels of personal integrity. Passion and enthusiasm for their goal is tantamount to their success, and when the "defense" of life is standing against them, they push forward and stretch for that next first down.

Do you have what it takes to win? Are you willing to work hard and be persistent? Traits like perseverance, humility, integrity, passion, and enthusiasm can turn you into a winner. Evaluate yourself and begin working on areas where you fall short.

SCORE A TOUCHDOWN!

You can develop the attributes of a winner. Not everyone is born with all the aforementioned characteristics, but you can grow in these areas. First, you need to believe in yourself and make a list of the type of person you want to become. Next, place yourself in situations where you will be challenged to cultivate your personal fortitude, character, and integrity.

Once you have a plan for self-improvement, begin to put it in action. Trust yourself. You can develop all the traits of a winner, but it does take a concerted effort realized over time and focused on personal development. Remember the journey to victory will also be paved with hurdles and obstacles that will be part of your eventual success, don't let them frustrate you or cause you to quit. You need those difficult times to help cultivate you into a winner. Go Blue!

Make a list below of the top five attributes of a winner, and then rate yourself on that same characteristic, one being low and ten being high. Work to improve in any area where you scored low.

1. _____

2. _____

3. _____

4. _____

5. _____

BE SPECTACULAR TODAY

Del Duduit

October 27, 2001: Michigan 32, Iowa 26

MICHIGAN TRAILED THE UNIVERSITY OF Iowa 20–14 near the end of the third quarter. The Wolverines faced a third and goal with the ball on the 6-yard line. They did not want to settle for a field goal and give the Hawkeyes a moral victory at the goal line.

Quarterback John Navarre dropped back to pass and scanned the field. Wide receiver Marquise Walker was double-teamed by two Iowa defenders but somehow made his way to the right corner of the end zone. Navarre tossed the ball Walker's way, but it appeared to be too high. Miraculously, Walker, who was six feet, two inches tall, leaped into the air and snagged the ball with his right hand. His fingers initially touched the ball, and then he was able to secure it and pull it into his body as he crashed toward the ground. Touchdown!

Iowa had defended the play well, but there was no answer for this spectacular catch, which has been hailed as one of the best acrobatic receptions ever made in college football history. The grab gave the Wolverines a

21–20 lead and inspired them to take a 32–26 win over the Hawkeyes in the Big House.

Later that season, on September 8, 2001, against the University of Washington, Walker caught fifteen passes to set the record for Michigan for the most catches in one game. He tied his own mark against Ohio State a few weeks later. In the Washington game, Walker had 159 yards receiving and scored two touchdowns in the 23–18 loss. Against the Buckeyes, he had 160 yards and two TDs. Both were career highs for Walker. He went on to set additional career marks at Michigan, including the most career receptions in school history. During his senior season in 2001, he set a Michigan single-season total record with eighty-six catches in ten games. Both have since been broken. He also finished his career with four blocked punts. But he will always be remembered for his improbable catch against Iowa that propelled the Wolverines to victory.

What about you? Chances are you will never be faced with a third goal on the Michigan 6-yard line. But you have opportunities in everyday life to make an impact. Could you make a play like Walker made?

DRIVE TO THE GOAL

What obstacles in life have put two defenders on you? Perhaps you have a deadline looming at work, and the pressure is on to come through in the clutch. At the same time, you are faced with a personal situation you did not ask for, but you know fourth down is approaching. You are torn between the two. Work might bombard you to the point it is affecting your relationships with your family and friends. Or maybe you want a job promotion that you feel you deserve. Perhaps you want to take a special family vacation you have been thinking about for years, but money is tight.

GET BEHIND THE DEFENSE

We all face challenges in life, and we all have dreams. No one ever promised an easy way into the end zone. But there are times when you must position yourself behind the defensive backs and go up and make the catch. The odds may be against you, but you must rely on your ability and all the years of hard work and dedication.

You can pull down the football and make the score, but it won't be easy. You must possess the confidence in yourself to make the right decision and come down with the ball. You won't get it unless you go after it. Quit talking or fantasizing about the big play and get the job done. Nothing has ever been accomplished with only good intentions. Walker could have let the ball sail past him since it appeared to be overthrown. But he was determined to bring it down and was resolved to win.

You, too, can make a spectacular play. All you have to do is put in the effort and believe in yourself and your ability. Go Blue!

How can you make a positive impact?

_____

_____

_____

_____

_____

_____

_____

—ᴍ—

UPSET ALERT

Cyle Young

October 18, 1997: Iowa at Michigan

THE 1997 FOOTBALL SEASON FOR the University of
Michigan was a true storybook season, with all its ups and
downs and one potential upset that almost derailed the
Wolverines' national championship efforts.

Entering the game against the University of Iowa,
Michigan had climbed in the rankings from number
seventeen to number five. On the back of a loss the previous week to Ohio State, Iowa stumbled into the matchup
with a 4–1 record and a number eight ranking. The tenacity with which Michigan overcame the struggles in this
game would go on to define their entire season.

The first quarter was a scoreless defensive struggle. But
ninety-one seconds into the second quarter, Iowa running
back Tavian Banks broke through the line of scrimmage
and darted 53 yards to give Iowa a 7–0 lead. Michigan
responded later in the second with a 15-yard touchdown
pass by quarterback Brian Griese.

The tie wouldn't last for long. On Michigan's next possession, Griese threw the ball into the hands of Iowa

cornerback Ed Gibson at the Iowa 36. Gibson's momentum carried him all the way to the Michigan 1-yard line. One play later, the Hawkeyes took the lead. Michigan's next drive would end with a punt to close out the half.

But Iowa's All-American wide receiver Tim Dwight had a different score in mind for halftime. The Big Ten hundred-meter-dash champion received the punt and blasted through the unprepared Michigan punt coverage. Dwight may have stood only five feet, eight inches tall, but when he crossed the goal line, giving the Hawkeyes a 14-point halftime lead, his presence seemed to loom over the entire stadium of 106,000 fans.

Michigan's coach, Lloyd Carr, stirred his team during halftime. He reminded them to stay unified, play together, and believe in each other. Their halftime deficit was the first real challenge of the season, and how they responded to the adversity would define the team.

The Wolverines came out of the locker room ready to play the second half. A long drive ended in a Griese touchdown pass to receiver Russell Shaw. And with 2:55 remaining in the third quarter, Griese converted a fourth-and-goal on the Iowa 1-yard line. Michigan tied the game at 21.

But Tim "White Lightning" Dwight would make short work of the tied game. He received the next kickoff and returned it 72 yards to set up an Iowa field goal. The third quarter ended 24–21 with Iowa in the lead. No matter what Michigan attempted to do on the field, Dwight seemed to singlehandedly undo it in an instant. Iowa would go on to hold the lead until late in the fourth quarter, when Griese rolled right on a bootleg from the Iowa 2 and found tight end Jerame Tuman in the back of the end zone to regain the lead 28–24. Hawkeye quarterback Matt Sherman drove Iowa down the field in an attempt to win the game, but Michigan linebacker Sam Sword would seal the Wolverine victory with an interception with just thirty-three seconds left on the clock.

Michigan's championship hopes remained alive because the team stayed unified in their adversity. They even overcame the playmaking pestering of future NFL player Tim Dwight.

Do you have a Tim Dwight in your life? Someone who, no matter what you accomplish, upstages you? How do you get past this person's antics and focus on your own success?

OVERCOME YOUR ADVERSARY

The 1997 Wolverines overcame the Tim Dwight effect by staying focused and continuing to work their game plan. Remember to stay focused, and don't let someone else's success limit your own. Work your own game plan for your life, and eventually you will overcome your adversary and achieve your own goals.

SURPASS AN UPSTAGER

Sometimes in life, no matter what you do, you feel like there is someone who upstages you. If you have a success, they have a greater one. If you get a raise, they get a bigger one. If your child gets a scholarship, their child gets even more offers. Football teams and players experience those same frustrations on and off the field.

You don't have to let someone else's success keep you from achieving your own. To achieve your personal success, keep focused on your goals. Keep your eyes fixed on the prize ahead and don't get distracted by someone else's accomplishment. Those type of distractions will only slow you down or cause you to quit. Believe in yourself and push toward your target, and don't let an upstager stand in your way. Go Blue!

Do you have any upstagers in your life? How can you overcome them?

_____

_____

_____

_____

_____

_____

_____

_____

_____

_____

_____

_____

_____

_____

_____

_____

_____

_____

_____

_____

_____

_____

_____

FIND A SILVER LINING

Del Duduit

October 4, 2003: Iowa 30, Michigan 27

NO ONE ENJOYS LOSING. BUT it's a part of life.

If a baseball player has a batting average of .300, he is considered to be an excellent hitter. This means the player got a hit three out of ten times at bat or failed 70 percent of the time. Either way, the batter is considered to be effective.

In football, a loss means the other team was either better prepared or had several things go right for them on a given day. Many times, the better team loses because its players did not execute certain plays at critical times.

But a good coach or player will try to find a silver lining, or something positive, to take away from a defeat. It doesn't mean the loss is tolerated, but it is taken as a learning point along the way. There can always be one positive attribute to a loss. Such was the case when the University of Iowa knocked off the University of Michigan 30–27.

The Hawkeyes played the game of their lives. Wide receiver Calvin Davis had his best day for Iowa and caught seven passes for 60 yards and a touchdown. Ramon

Ochoa, a running back, whipped off 169 yards rushing and played a key role in 17 of the team's 30 points.

The only bright spot for Michigan that day was quarterback John Navarre, who set the school's single-game record for the most passing yards with 389—a record that stood for a decade until Devin Gardner threw for 503 yards against Indiana. Navarre played well for the Wolverines; for the season, he threw for 3,331 yards with twenty-four touchdowns and helped the team to win games over rivals Ohio State and Notre Dame. However, on October 4, 2003, Iowa played a little better. Navarre was the bright spot in the loss to Iowa.

Have you ever suffered a setback in life? Everyone does; what matters is how you handle it. Did you learn from a mistake and have something good come from the situation?

LOOK OVER THE GAME FILM

You may have been dealt a rough blow in the past. Perhaps you were laid off from your job or you experienced some health problems. Maybe you were not treated fairly in a relationship or had to deal with some unpleasant personal or family issues. No matter what negative experiences you have had to cope with, you must move forward. One loss does not ruin the entire season. Michigan went on to play in the granddaddy of them all that year—the Rose Bowl—even after a heartbreaking loss.

PREPARE FOR THE NEXT GAME

There are silver linings to take away from most defeats. Navarre set a school record in the game against Iowa.

Would he rather have won and thrown for fewer yards? Probably. But he shone bright that day, even though the team went down in points. He tried and put forth a valiant effort. A victory was just not meant to be on that Saturday.

When you have a bad day, will your life be turned upside down? It could be. But it's how you respond to negativity that allows you to go on to play in the Rose Bowl. If you let losing get the best of you, then you might give up, quit, and walk into the locker room dejected. Instead, think about what happened and the reasons why, and try to find something positive that can come out of the loss. Build on the experience, and work to make sure it doesn't happen again. If you did something wrong, try harder next time, and don't repeat the mistake. Take note of the good things that have emerged, and be determined to have a winning season. Put the loss behind you, and move on to the next game.

You can overcome a setback or loss. You must be resilient and stay tough. Be willing to change, and stay prepared and focused on your goal. Reward yourself when you experience a small victory, and pick yourself up after a loss. Always learn and be positive. Accept the defeat and look ahead to the next Saturday matchup. Michigan rebounded and knocked off Minnesota the next week 38–35. You can do the same. Go Blue!

What lessons have you learned from your mistakes?

_____

_____

_____

_____

_____

SNOW BOWL

Cyle Young

November 25, 1950: Michigan at Ohio State

THE UNIVERSITY OF MICHIGAN HAS a unique way of ruining Ohio State University's seasons. It's what makes the rivalry so great, and Ohio State is happy to return the favor when Michigan is having an excellent championship-quality season.

In 1950, Ohio State entered the rivalry game as number eight in the country. They were well on their way to the overall Big Ten Conference title. Then a blizzard hit Columbus. The game on November 25 started almost two and a half hours late because four feet of snow had fallen on top of the tarp covering the field. Ohio State groundskeepers had to recruit local Boy Scouts and fans to help get the snow and tarp off the field.

Over 50,000 fans still showed up to brave the ten-degree weather and thirty-mile-an-hour winds to watch Michigan play Ohio State. But on the icy field, there wouldn't be much to watch that day—unless you were thrilled with a lot of punts.

Both teams' offenses struggled. Michigan ran forty-six plays for a total of 27 yards, and the Buckeyes ran fifty-eight offensive plays for a total of 41 yards gained. Michigan kickers totaled 685 yards on twenty-one kicks, and Ohio State kickers topped that total with 724 yards kicked on twenty-four attempts. The kick returners weren't as successful for either team. Michigan managed only 47 return yards, and Ohio State mustered only 29 return yards total.

Over the course of the game, Michigan and Ohio State punted forty-five times—often on first down. The teams decided it was easier to punt on first down and hope that the opponent would fumble the return.

Every score in the game was the result of a blocked punt. Ohio State defensive lineman Bob Momsen blocked a punt and recovered it at the Michigan 8-yard line. It was Michigan's only blocked punt of the game. But the Ohio State offense couldn't convert the excellent field position into a touchdown. Instead, they lost 13 yards on the next three plays and settled for a 38-yard field goal and a 3-point lead.

The Michigan defense responded to the score by blocking four of Ohio State's Heisman Trophy–winning halfback Vic Janowicz's punts. One of those blocked punts resulted in a safety for the Buckeyes as the ball rolled out of the end zone. Michigan would later score at the end of the first half when Wolverine Tony Momsen—brother of Ohio State's Bob Momsen—blocked a punt and recovered it in the end zone to give the Wolverines a 9–3 lead.

The game would end with that final score, and Michigan would win the Big Ten Conference and gain a trip to the Rose Bowl, where they would go on to beat California

14–6 and finish number six in the country's final football poll.

Michigan wasn't going to let a little weather stand in the way of a Big Ten championship. Sure, they had to change their tactics to win. Punting on a first down is never a standard football strategy, but they pulled off the win and won a trip to the Rose Bowl.

If you are facing a blizzard in your life, how can you change your game plan to allow you to overcome the odds and have success?

CHANGE THE GAME PLAN

Sometimes in life you may need to change your strategy a little. Blizzards come in many forms, in relationships, in workplaces, and in all facets of life. You can't tackle every problem the same way, and you can't always score by using the same strategy.

FIND A WAY TO WIN

Life throws blizzards at you from time to time. Situations at home, work, or school that are so overwhelming that you don't see a clear path to victory. Accomplishing any task during life's blizzard can be extremely difficult. But just because the task is hard doesn't mean you can't achieve your goals. Some of Michigan football's most legendary games have been in actual blizzards. Players' hands were so stiff and frozen they couldn't catch or pass, or even hold on to the football—but they found a way to win, and you can too.

Know that you are not alone. You are not the only person to ever face strenuous times. Others have overcome overwhelming odds and found great victory. Oprah Winfrey grew up in poverty and at the age of 14 lost a child shortly after his birth. Steve Jobs was forced out of his own company. Both Orpah and Steve determined they wouldn't let their circumstances control their destiny. Be tenacious and you too can achieve your greatest feat, even when faced with great difficulty. Go Blue!

How have you overcome blizzards in your life in the past? What's your game plan for dealing with setbacks in the future?"

———————————————————————
———————————————————————
———————————————————————
———————————————————————
———————————————————————
———————————————————————
———————————————————————
———————————————————————
———————————————————————
———————————————————————
———————————————————————
———————————————————————
———————————————————————
———————————————————————
———————————————————————
———————————————————————
———————————————————————
———————————————————————
———————————————————————
———————————————————————

BE VERSATILE FOR YOUR TEAM

Del Duduit

December 5, 2016: Michigan 59, Maryland 3

MICHIGAN FANS HAD A GEM in Jabrill Peppers. The multipurpose athlete was regarded by many as one of the best players in college football. On this day, he showed why he was amazing.

Peppers lined up as a wide receiver and went in motion across the right side of the field. The ball was snapped, and quarterback Wilton Speight handed it off to Peppers. The defense initially thought it was a sweep around the corner, but Peppers pulled up and fired the ball across the field back to Speight. The quarterback then launched a bomb to Jehu Chesson, who caught the ball and set up another score as the number three ranked Wolverines trounced Maryland 59–3 in the Big House.

Peppers had once again shown his versatility. During his career, the Heisman nominee played eleven different positions. Most players on a college roster might see action in two or three roles, but never in the double digits. He was special.

Coach Jim Harbaugh said on a regular basis that Peppers was one of the best all-around players he had ever seen. Let's examine all the ways he contributed to his team. Over his tenure at Michigan, he played quarterback in the Wildcat formation several times. On one occasion, he took a busted play and scampered 63 yards to set up an easy score against Rutgers. He served as a running back and an H-back to spread the defense out. He played wide receiver and returned punts and kickoffs. On defense, he played cornerback, the nickel back, safety, and linebacker. He was so good and effective as a backer that he led the team with fifteen tackles for a loss. And finally, Peppers was even used to block punts for Michigan. His helmet had the most Wolverine decals on it because he played hard and took on any position the team needed him in to win.

What do you bring to your team? How many skills do you have?

PLAY YOUR POSITION

To do a task well is admirable. If you can be one of the best employees in your company, that's fantastic. Dedication to completing a task is a great and admirable characteristic. When you stay loyal to your spouse and to yourself, then you cannot ask for anything more from a person. But can you do more? Is there a piece of you that longs to contribute to worthwhile causes? Can you play multiple positions?

EXPAND YOUR PLAYBOOK

There is more to life than work and play. You have obligations, and you meet them. But a busy person gets more done. You were put on this earth to do good. Your first goal is to be a productive and moral person. But you also have a deep desire to set an example for others.

Don't put limits on yourself. Instead, explore avenues to broaden your horizons and become a valuable member of your team. This is important both at work and at home. Become involved in a charitable organization and give back to your community. Consider a volunteer coaching position, or mentor a child as a Big Brother or Big Sister. Be a parent who is involved in your children's activities, but don't hover and take control. Consider helping those less fortunate than you or spending time at a food shelter on a regular basis.

This life is not just about work. It's about being versatile and meeting the needs of those around you. You have many skills you may not even know about. Take time to examine yourself and what talents you possess. If you have a strong personality, consider being a person who asks for donations to help a worthy cause. Perhaps you have a soft spot in your heart. Then maybe taking clothes to a Salvation Army should be on your to-do list. You can also be effective in helping find homes for stray animals.

There are countless ways you can better your community and life. Peppers could play any position on his team. He adapted and performed at a high level. You can do the same in your life. Go Blue!

What are your best skills, and how to do you use them for good?

_____

_____

_____

_____

_____

SPRING GAME

Cyle Young

April 2, 2016: Michigan at Michigan

A SPRING GAME ISN'T USUALLY considered to be one of the greatest moments in a team's football history. Or at least if it is, the team probably isn't any good, and definitely not the winningest football program in sports history. However, the 2016 Spring Game was a sight to behold.

University of Michigan coach Jim Harbaugh loves spectacle. Over the course of the previous recruiting season, he'd managed to pull together one of the nation's top recruiting classes. And the exclamation point on his success was the number one recruit in the country, New Jersey's Paramus Catholic five-star defensive tackle Rashan Gary. Gary had received offers from every major football team in the country, but he chose Michigan to be his home.

The Spring Game came on the heels of Harbaugh's signing day spectacular in February, dubbed the Signing of the Stars. Three thousand fans filled the Hill Auditorium in Ann Arbor to watch. NFL future Hall of Famer Tom

Brady announced three recruits; MLB legend Derek Jeter announced two recruits onstage; and Baltimore Ravens head coach John Harbaugh and WWE Superstar Ric Flair also participated in the event as well as Michigan rappers and other celebrities. It was a sight to behold.

The months leading up to the Spring Game built anticipation upon anticipation. And in Jim Harbaugh fashion, the game featured yet another spectacle. During halftime, the 2016 recruits paraded onto the field one at a time. Cheers erupted in the stadium, and loud music played leading up to the announcement of the final member of the class: Rashan Gary.

Standing on the edge of the end zone, Gary twirled slowly, taking it all in. When his name was announced, he raised his arms and strutted from the end zone like a proud peacock, between two parallel rows of dancers and cheerleaders shaking their pom-poms.

Gary and the nation's fifth-best recruiting class gave the Michigan faithful hope. After 2015 losses to both Michigan State and Ohio State, Wolverine fans wanted something to get excited about. The 10–3 season was the start of the next phase of Michigan football. Harbaugh's new recruits would help him reestablish a winning tradition after his predecessors had failed to bring consistent championships to the University of Michigan. The tide was beginning to turn. Harbaugh was a Michigan man who bled Maize and Blue, and he would continue to right the ship.

What gives you hope in the face of adversity? Are you able to rally your team, overcome setbacks, and head for a winning season?

EMBRACE A NEW HOPE

Do you need the kind of hope in your life that the 2016 recruiting class inspired in Michigan fans? Are you struggling to have a positive attitude or outlook on the future? You don't have to. Seasons come and seasons go, in life just like in football. This season of despair or disappointment will eventually end, and you will be able to embrace the excitement of new beginnings.

CHANGE YOUR GAME PLAN

You may not be able to land the number one recruit in the country, but you can carve out your own ways to change your circumstances. Start something new. Find your passion and then follow it to new adventures in your life. Connect with others who will support and encourage you on your journey. Commit to hard work. You can't change your game plan without a little blood and sweat. Take action each day to change your circumstances and over time the direction of your life will be fully under your control. Go Blue!

Make a list of three things you can do right now to begin to change your outlook.

1. _____
2. _____
3. _____

A GOOD DEFENSE WINS GAMES

Del Duduit

November 25, 1989: Michigan 28, Ohio State 18

TODD PLATE AND ERICK ANDERSON wreaked havoc on the Ohio State University offense and made sure the Wolverines won the rivalry game 28–18 in the Big House. Plate picked off two Buckeye passes; Anderson ravaged the running game and had twelve solo tackles and fifteen in all from his linebacker position. Both of the players' efforts propelled Michigan to its second straight Big Ten championship and a trip to the coveted Rose Bowl.

Plate's interceptions came in the fourth quarter and kept Ohio State from taking the lead in the final stanza. The Buckeyes trailed 14–12 when Plate made his first theft. The second one came with 3:30 left to play, and OSU was driving at midfield. He broke on a pass meant for Buckeye receiver Greg Beatty and took the ball away for the Wolverines. Two minutes later, the Maize and Blue scored on a 23-yard run by Jarrod Bunch to put the game out of reach.

Meanwhile, Anderson, a sophomore, had one of the best games of his four-year career in the middle of the defense. He is regarded as one of the best linebackers ever to play in Michigan. During his senior year, he won the prestigious Butkus Award, given to the best collegiate linebacker in the country. He was also the Co-Defensive Player of the Year in the Big Ten and was first team All-American. He led the team in tackles all four years at Michigan and never lost to Ohio State.

You won't face your archrival just once a year like Michigan does when it plays the Buckeyes every November. Your battles come daily. The start of each new day brings opportunities for you to tackle your opponent and make key interceptions from life's difficulties to allow you to win the game.

Do you find yourself with your guard up a lot during the day? You might have good reason to display a solid self-defense, but be careful not to let that habit define you.

LINE UP THE DEFENSE

Have you ever been rejected from the job of a lifetime? Perhaps you have been placed in a social setting that made you feel uncomfortable. Or maybe you had an argument with your spouse or a close friend. You are not alone. Life is full of negative situations, and you have to come up with a plan to defend yourself from and attack them. Frustrations in life are unavoidable, but during these times you can discover what you are made of and examine how you react under pressure. You cannot let situations run you over.

GO FOR THE BLITZ

We all defend ourselves. It's human nature. But for most people, a lousy situation will unleash protective measures to deal with unplanned emotions. How you cope with a negative situation will say a lot about your character. When a bad moment occurs, try to notice if your defense mechanism asserts itself and impedes your progression in life.

How do you handle moments of pressure? What do you do when life calls for a blitz on your well-calculated plans? Some of your emotions might include denial, displacement, rationalization, sublimation, and repression. You might deny that a circumstance ever happened and refuse to accept the outcome. You might experience displacement if you have a bad day and come home and kick your dog. He didn't do anything to deserve the result of your frustration, but he was in the wrong place at the wrong time. You might rationalize your behavior, which is when you make excuses and justifications for your actions. Sublimation happens when you transfer your anger into another outlet. You might become agitated at work and then go to the gym and take it out on a punching bag or run a few miles. Or perhaps you repress the entire situation from your mind—you block it out and act as if it never happened.

There are better methods to deal with life's unpleasant circumstances. The best offense is a good defense. Take responsibility, and examine why something took place. Don't let your defense mechanisms take over the game. Never make excuses for what happens in your life. Instead, analyze your behavior, and keep the ball moving toward the goal line. A defense mechanism can be a good thing at times, but in the fourth quarter when the game is on the line, you don't want it to control your life. Stay calm, and go Blue!

What three ways do you take responsibility?

FALL SEASON

INTERIM

Cyle Young

August 27, 1995: Virginia at Michigan

THE 1994 SEASON WAS UNSATISFYING for the Wolverines. During one of the key games in the 1994 season, University of Colorado's Kordell Stewart lofted a desperate Hail Mary pass in the final moments of the game to give the Buffaloes the surprise win. The Wolverines went on to finish the season a disappointing 8–4.

Enter interim head coach Lloyd Carr and the Pigskin Classic. For a period of twelve years (1990–2002), the NCAA allowed an extra twelfth game at the beginning of the season if the first game were a licensed "Classic." In 1995, the University of Michigan hosted the University of Virginia for the Pigskin Classic in Ann Arbor.

The opening game against Virginia gave Coach Carr the national stage to spotlight his team and make a statement to college football voters. Not only did the Wolverines have a new coach, they were also starting a freshman quarterback for the first time since 1976. Scott Dreisbach was as untested as his new coach, and the Virginia game would reveal what kind of quarterback he was going to be.

Virginia stormed out to a lead early and, with twelve minutes to go in the fourth quarter, held on to a 17–0 lead. Michigan's quarterback struggled throughout the game, throwing two interceptions with a less than stellar completion percentage.

Boos rained from the audience. Fans wanted to see another quarterback get a shot in the final minutes. A backup had to be better than Dreisbach. But Coach Carr stuck to his guns. "The most important decision I made was when I stayed with Dreisbach," he said. "There's no question when you have all inexperienced guys, the guy who has played the last 48 minutes for you, he gives you the best chance to win."

Down 17–0, Michigan drove down the field and scored on a 2-yard touchdown by running back Ed Davis. The Michigan crowd settled down. Dreisbach had managed to put a drive together. The defense held on the next Virginia series, and when the Wolverines regained possession of the ball, Dreisbach led the team down the field again, capping the drive with a 31-yard touchdown pass to Mercury Hayes.

After Michigan failed to convert its extra points, all Virginia needed was a field goal to seal the win. They drove down the field, but on a critical third and two near midfield, one of the Virginia linemen missed a crucial block, and the Michigan defense stopped the Cavaliers. Dreisbach and the Wolverines would have a chance to win the game.

The Cavaliers punted the ball, and Michigan regained possession at their 20-yard line. With 2:35 left on the clock, the Wolverines had plenty of time to drive the 80 yards to score. It took them sixteen plays and 2:31 to get to the Virginia 15-yard line. With four seconds left in the contest, Michigan had one play left—a fourth down play.

With time expiring on the clock, Dreisbach found Hayes in the back corner of the end zone. Hayes managed to barely get one foot down in bounds as he made the catch between two Cavalier defenders. When the field judge signaled touchdown, the stadium roared. Michigan took over the lead 18–17. Coach Carr and the Wolverines had overcome the boos, sealing one of the greatest come-from-behind victories in Michigan football history. Dreisbach also set Michigan passing records that day—fifty-two attempts and 372 passing yards were both new standards for the Wolverines.

Despite all the criticism, Scott Dreisbach led his team to a great victory. Likewise, Coach Carr stuck to his guns. He could have easily replaced the freshman quarterback with a backup, but Carr knew the game plan, and he knew his players. The new head coach didn't have to make changes to his personnel just because the crowd thought they knew better. He could have appeased the fans with a change, but the Wolverines would have probably gone on to lose the game.

The Pigskin Classic would go on to define the 1995 season, and many believe that the win over an impressive Cavalier squad placed the interim coach securely in the lead for the permanent head coach position, even though Michigan Athletic Director Joe Roberson had previously stated the Carr would not be a candidate for the full-time position. Carr also believed the game solidified him becoming head coach, saying "My guess is had we not won that game I would have never become the head coach at Michigan. From that standpoint, it was a pretty important decision for me."

What do you do when others' opinions differ from your own? Do you give in and change, or do you stick to your game plan?

OVERCOME BOOS AND JEERS

Have you ever felt like the world was against you? That no matter what you tried to accomplish, people seemed to boo you and complain about your skill, ability, or effort? Many times, those jeers come from the people who are supposed to be your biggest fans. But don't let their comments get to you. Stick to your guns. If you know you are making the right decisions, or if you know you are giving your best effort, then don't listen to the naysayers. You will never please everyone, and you don't want to miss out on amazing personal victories because you tried to please a few disgruntled people.

STICK WITH YOUR GAME PLAN

The best way to stick with your game plan is to have a short memory. You have to forget mistakes, mess-ups, and problems as quickly as possible. Don't let them become a focus point. The sooner you let those negative things leave your memory banks the happier you will be, and the more productive you will be toward reaching your goals in relationships, at work, or at home. Go Blue!

Do you have a short memory for mistakes? Or do you hang on to bad things way too long? How can you improve in this area?

_____

_____

_____

_____

_____

_____

WHAT DOES YOUR NICKNAME SAY ABOUT YOU?

Del Duduit

September 18, 1943: Michigan 26, United States Army 0

THERE'S "HONEST ABE" LINCOLN. WHO remembers Andrew "Old Hickory" Jackson? What about John "The Duke" Wayne? Every University of Michigan fan knows who Denard "Shoelace" Robinson is in the school's storied history.

All earned their nicknames because of their unique style or a characteristic they possessed. President Lincoln was noted to always be truthful, while Jackson had a reputation as a tough guy. And the legendary actor received his nickname because he spent so much time with his dog named Duke that the pair was called "Little Duke" and "Big Duke." Robinson earned his nickname because he never tied his shoelaces.

The first game of the 1943 season featured a fantastic performance by Elroy "Crazylegs" Hirsch. He set the tone early when he returned the opening kickoff 50 yards. He later scored on a 3-yard run in the first quarter. Before the first half was over, he ran for another touchdown. Michigan's final score of the game was set up when Hirsch picked off an Army pass. He led the Wolverines' offensive attack that rushed for 226 yards and passed for 138.

How did Hirsch earn his nickname, "Crazylegs"? According to many reports, it was because of his unusual running style and the way his long legs twisted from side to side. One sportswriter from the *Chicago Daily News* described his method of running as "gyrating in six different directions, all at the same time." The writer also used the phrase "crazy legs" in his story. There were other reports of how Hirsch obtained the name, but it didn't matter. When the sportswriter noted Hirsch's "crazy legs," it caught on, and people referred to him that way throughout his career. This was okay with him; in fact, it's said he preferred it to his given name, Elroy.

What have you done in your life to earn a nickname? Do you even have one? If not, think about the topic going forward. If you had to pick a phrase or nickname to describe yourself, what would it be?

DRAW UP THE PLAY

Have you earned a nickname you do not find flattering? Have you developed a reputation you desire to be changed? There are many words you want to stay away from when people describe you or your attitude. You never want to have your name and the following words in the same sentence: *lazy, incompetent, irresponsible, useless, grumpy, untruthful, sneaky, two-faced, snarky, quicktempered, hateful, mean, spiteful, inconsiderate, late, bitter, cheater, selfish, cold* . . . and the list could continue.

Maybe you have done things to bring about some of these descriptions. Realize there is time to start over and change. Hirsch actually began his college career at the University of Wisconsin, where he was an All-American football player. But he enlisted in the US Marine Corps and was later transferred to Michigan as part of the V-12 Navy College Training Program. He started over.

GAIN THE FIRST DOWN

If you feel the need to begin anew and give people a reason to refer to you in a positive light, you can. It is never too late to start fresh. Whether circumstances in life have caused you to act certain ways, it doesn't matter. When you turn over a new leaf and possess a different attitude, people will take note.

Strive to be described by others with some of these words: *kind, reliable, considerate, dependable, honest, sensible, a go-getter, helpful, thoughtful, sincere, honorable, capable, courageous, affectionate, loyal, amiable, adventurous, exuberant, generous, passionate, practical,* and *fun.* You may be able to come up with more positive words to describe yourself. The point here is that it is never too late to reinvent yourself. Take on the right attitude and go for the end zone. Remember, this might take some time. But also know the college football season is long for one reason—to give the team another chance to win each week. Go Blue!

What three words best describe you?

_____

_____
_____

_____

_____

—⚏—

THE GAME

Cyle Young

November 25, 1995: Ohio State at Michigan

ELEVEN DAYS AFTER INTERIM COACH Lloyd Carr had been named the permanent head coach at the University of Michigan, his Wolverines welcomed the undefeated Ohio State University, the number two team in the country, to Michigan Stadium.

The Buckeyes rolled into Ann Arbor with one of the best offensive teams they'd ever put together. Running back Eddie George would go on to win the Heisman Trophy due to his impressive season of 1,927 rushing and 417 receiving yards, with twenty-four rushing touchdowns. But George wasn't Ohio State's only superstar. Wide receiver Terry Glenn compiled 1,411 receiving yards and seventeen touchdowns in the season.

For all intents and purposes, the Buckeyes intended to steamroll their way through Ann Arbor on their way to a potential national championship. Before the game, Ohio State's Glenn famously quipped, "Michigan is nobody. I guarantee we're going to the Rose Bowl." That's all the ammo the Wolverines needed to fire them up.

Ohio State would score first, going up 3–0 on a field goal late in the first quarter. Michigan answered with a touchdown on the next possession. They would never fall behind again. George and Glenn both turned in mild statistical performances. George rushed for 104 yards, his second lowest total of the season, and Glenn caught four passes for 72 yards.

But the Wolverines were another story. Michigan running back Tshimanga Biakabutuka slashed the Buckeyes' defense, gaining 313 yards on thirty-seven carries. Freshman cornerback and Ohio native Charles Woodson intercepted two passes by Buckeye quarterback Bobby Hoying. His second interception sealed the win, stalling Ohio State's final drive with forty-eight seconds left.

After the game, Ohio State coach John Cooper shared, "I'm tremendously disappointed. I don't know if I've ever been as disappointed as I am right now." Michigan and Ohio State would both go on to lose their respective bowl games, but Michigan ended their season on a high note by beating their hated rivals and ruining their championship season.

It didn't matter how much star power the Buckeyes had; Michigan had everything to gain and nothing to lose. Add that to the pregame disrespect by the Buckeye players, and it was all the kindling needed to build an upset bonfire.

Have you ever been counted out? Disrespected by a person or society? What did you do in response?

RALLY FOR AN UPSET

No one likes to be marginalized or discounted. But just because other people don't see your value, it doesn't mean you can't rise to great success. The 1995 Wolverines are a prime example. The Ohio State game was the second time during that season when football pundits didn't believe Michigan could win. And both times the Wolverines proved them wrong—and in drastic fashion.

Other people don't define you or your success. You have to start believing the right things about yourself to overcome disrespect. Once you believe in yourself you can attain whatever goal you've set for yourself, even though the odds may be stacked against you.

STAY IN THE GAME

When you've been counted out, you can overcome with specific strategies engineered to give you a leg up on the competition. One of the best strategies is to outhustle and outwork your naysayers. Hard work pays off. The adage, work smarter not harder is a good mantra to put your faith in. If you look at your situation from a different perspective, you may be able to uncover a new way to tackle your problem or conquer your adversary. Go Blue!

Make a list below of some negative comments people have made about you, and then write what you know to be true next to it.

Negative: **Positive:**

_____   _____

_____   _____

_____   _____

_____   _____

BE ACCOUNTABLE

Del Duduit

October 3, 1925; Michigan 39, Michigan State 0

ONE PLAYER CAN MAKE A difference.

The game of football is geared toward teamwork. Hours of preparation go into each game. If one person does not do their assigned job, the entire designed goal is at risk. When all players work as one unit, they can accomplish meaningful results.

But on occasion, an individual comes along who stands out in the crowd. Each team may produce a star player who rises to the top. This is not meant in a negative or condescending way toward the other participants; it's part of the game.

When Benny Friedman moved from his halfback position to quarterback in 1925, it was evident he was special and was meant to be a leader. In the season opener against rival Michigan State, the junior did it all. He scored a touchdown on a 65-yard run and later connected with Bruce Gregory for a 30-yard TD pass. Then, in the second half, Friedman intercepted a Spartan pass on defense.

On offense, he found Bennie Oosterbaan for a 24-yard scoring strike.

But he didn't have just one amazing game. In University of Michigan's 63–0 romp over Indiana, he accounted for 50 points. He threw five touchdown passes, ran for one, and kicked two field goals and eight extra points. And he didn't stop there. He guided Michigan to a 21–0 thumping over University of Wisconsin, where he threw for a 62-yard touchdown and returned a kickoff 85 yards for a score.

Friedman kept up the pace and led the Wolverines to a lopsided 54–0 win over Navy, where he tossed two touchdown passes and kicked five extra points. In the final game of the season, Friedman led Michigan to a 35–0 victory over University of Minnesota for the Wolverines' seventh shutout in eight games. History records that he completed thirty-four of eighty-three passes and had thirteen touchdowns for the year. On the defensive end, he racked up eight interceptions and was selected as a first-team All-American.

Benny Friedman is regarded as one of Michigan's greatest all-round players. He made sure he did his job on the field to make his team better. Not everyone can be the superstar, and not every team needs one. What every squad must have is people who carry their load. When everyone does what they are expected to do, good things are more likely to happen. Is this a guarantee? Not at all. But it does improve their chances of winning the game. When teammates join forces and do the little things in life, it adds up and matters in the end. Teamwork wins games.

What do you do to help? Are you a standout on the job or just another number? Can you make a difference at home or on your team? Or are you content to stand on the sidelines?

HUDDLE UP TOGETHER

Maybe you have landed your dream job or convinced a large client to sign on the dotted line. Or perhaps the girl you've courted for years said "yes" to your proposal. What's next? In reality, when these events happen, it signals the beginning rather than a culmination of hard work and dedication. Now you have a commitment to follow and responsibilities ahead. The game has just started and the kicker put the ball in the air.

EXECUTE YOUR ASSIGNMENT

Your game plan is straightforward and easy. You do not have to be the superstar for your team in order to win. Focus on your job, and contribute in simple ways. A smile and a laugh can pick up a person who is down. Humor can be contagious, and you can be the reason your office or family is in a better mood.

You can also volunteer your time and help someone who is less fortunate than you. Never consider it pity, but develop the attitude that you want to lend a hand and pick someone up. Who knows? You may be on the other end and need help one day. If you can't afford the time, you can donate to causes with clothing, food, or money.

Make sure you focus on others and put their needs ahead of yours. This does not mean you should neglect your work or family, but you can make time for other activities once your obligations are met. When you make yourself valuable to other people and let them know how much you care, you will be considered the most dependable person on your team.

Benny Friedman did it all. He ran, passed, kicked, and just about everything else he could do to lead the Wolverines to victory. Don't limit yourself to one or two good deeds. Go all out and find ways to win. Go Blue!

How are you accountable?

_____

_____

_____

_____

_____

_____

_____

_____

_____

_____

_____

_____

_____

_____

_____

_____

_____

_____

_____

_____

THE CONTROVERSY

Cyle Young

November 24, 1973: Ohio State at Michigan

AN NCAA RECORD CROWD OF 105,233 showed up in Ann Arbor to watch the number four University of Michigan Wolverines host the number one Ohio State Buckeyes. The winner of the game would represent the Big Ten Conference in the Rose Bowl as Big Ten champions. The victor would also have the opportunity to be crowned college football's national champion.

Each team entered the game ready to spoil the other's season. Quarterback Cornelius Greene led the Buckeye offense, but it was future two-time Heisman Trophy winner Archie Griffin who made it click. The Buckeyes also possessed one of college football's greatest right tackles, John Hicks, who was the last offensive lineman to place second in the Heisman Trophy race.

Michigan was a running team. Five different players recorded over 400 rushing yards in the season. Running back Ed Shuttlesworth topped the list with 745 yards on 193 attempts. The weather played to both teams' strength: running the ball. Rain pounded the turf, and both teams struggled to find the scoreboard in the first quarter. Ohio State would eventually get a second-quarter field goal to go up 3–0. Archie Griffin would tally 99 rushing yards in the first half, and eventually Buckeye fullback Pete Johnson would find the end zone to give the Buckeyes a 10–0 lead.

Michigan coach Bo Schembechler had to make some significant halftime adjustments to slow down the Buckeye rushing attack. When the Wolverines exited the tunnel, they were ready. In the second half, Michigan outgained the Buckeyes 209 yards to 91. Archie Griffin was held to just 65 more yards on offense. Early in the fourth quarter, the Wolverines made a field goal to bring the game within seven.

Midway through the fourth, Michigan sustained a drive deep into Ohio State territory. On a fourth-and-inches, Franklin slipped between the linemen for a game-tying quarterback sneak. On the Wolverines' next position, Franklin was leading the team down the field when he was hit while throwing a pass. The hard collision broke his collarbone. Two plays later, Michigan kicker Mike Lantry missed a 58-yard field goal attempt to win the game. Neither Michigan nor Ohio State could capitalize in the final minutes, and Michigan would miss another field goal attempt to win the game.

The two juggernaut football teams had entered the game undefeated and then left the game the same way— still undefeated, but with a tie. The real rub for the Wolverines came after the game had concluded. The Big Ten Conference athletic directors cast secret ballots to determine which team should represent the conference in the Rose Bowl. All fairness would suggest it was the

Wolverines' turn, since Ohio State had represented the conference the previous year in the game. In a surprise decision, Ohio State was chosen—again.

Coach Schembechler turned to the media to share his frustration and disappointment. Many theories have been proposed about which athletic directors voted for which team and why, but it's obvious Franklin's injury played an important role in the decision as well as the fact that the Big Ten Conference had lost the last four Rose Bowls, and they wanted to field the best, most competitive team.

No matter why the Wolverines weren't chosen, the decision wasn't fair. Schembechler would successfully push to change the Rose Bowl selection process in subsequent years, but it wouldn't retroactively fix the unfairness that his team suffered in 1973.

OVERCOME UNFAIRNESS

The 1973 decision against the University of Michigan was unfair, but it was a reality the Wolverines had to deal with. That year lives on as one of Michigan's greatest football teams, but there will always be a sting surrounding the end of the season.

Have you ever experienced this sort of unfairness in your life? Maybe your coworker received a promotion you deserved, someone else's child was chosen over yours for an elite traveling sports team, or a friend won the lottery on his first attempt, but you've been playing for years and haven't won anything.

Whatever the unfairness, it hurts. But like the 1973 Wolverines, you must learn to live with it. Just because life isn't fair, it doesn't mean it isn't worth living. Life is great, and even though everything doesn't always go your way, there's still tomorrow—more great opportunities are just around the corner.

OVERCOME DISAPPOINTMENT

When things don't go your way the first step is to breathe. Just breathe. Release the tension and stress building up inside and clear your mind. A cloudy mind will cause you to act out emotionally and irrationally. To reach your objective, you must be able to rationally make decisions even in the midst of great disappointment. Once your breath and thoughts are under your control, you are ready to push on. Momentary setbacks are always frustrating, but you don't have to let them defeat you. Let those hurdles drive you toward an even bigger goal. Go Blue!

Have you ever been so stressed that your breathing changes? How can you calm yourself in these moments?

DELIVER IN A BIG WAY

Del Duduit

October 19, 2013: Michigan 63, Indiana 47

UNIVERSITY OF MICHIGAN WIDE RECEIVER Jeremy Gallon enjoyed a tremendous day in the Big House. The senior hauled in a whopping fourteen catches and accounted for an incredible 369 yards as he led the Wolverines over Indiana University 63–47. His performance set a Big Ten Conference record and ranked second all-time in NCAA D-I history in the Football Bowl Subdivision.

Quarterback Devin Gardner also turned in a tremendous performance, finishing the day with twenty-one of twenty-nine completions for 503 yards—also a Michigan record—and two touchdowns. He carried the ball fifteen times for 81 yards and three scores.

The third quarter was pure offense for both schools as they combined for 38 points. Michigan later drove all the way to the Hoosier 2-yard line, but Gardner lost a fumble to Indiana. A few plays later, Michigan's Tom Gordon picked off an Indiana pass and took it to the 5-yard line. Two plays later, Gardner redeemed his goof when he dove into the end zone for the 56–47 lead with 6:01 to go in the game.

The Wolverines would break the school record for total offense in one game on a 27-yard touchdown run by Fitz Toussaint, his fourth of the day. Gallon was a one-man wrecking machine for the Wolverines. He caught eight passes from Gardner for 170 yards in the first half. But it was not rare for Gallon to put up big numbers. In 2011, he was the team's leading receiver through the first four games. On September 10, 2011, he caught two passes for 78 yards, which included a 64-yard catch late in the game that set up a Michigan score and the game-winning touchdown. In a big victory over Northwestern University a few weeks later, he caught five passes for 73 yards, which featured a 25-yard screen play for a score.

During the season, he was Michigan's second leading receiver with thirty catches for 450 yards and three touchdowns. He was also the team's leading punt returner with nineteen returns for 192 yards, an average of 10.1 yards per return. The next year, he was the team's leading receiver with forty-nine catches for 829 yards and four scores. He had a solid history of being a big-time producer on the field and piled up several awards.

What do you contribute? Can you be depended on to produce?

VISUALIZE GAME DAY

Imagine it's your first day of work. You might be a little nervous or apprehensive because you want to fit in and make a good impression. Or maybe it's your first date with someone you like. You want the evening to go smoothly and possibly lead to another night out on the town. Or maybe you are in the waiting room and anticipating your firstborn child. What goes through your mind? What do you want to accomplish with this new adventure?

GET THE JOB DONE

No matter what you face, you want to do your best and be regarded as a person who is dependable and makes good decisions. Instead of making the 64-yard catch, you want to make a good living and leave a legacy as a producer.

There are several ways you can accomplish these goals. First you must realize it's not about money but rather about character and integrity. Don't be too critical of yourself. Toss any guilty feelings you have out the window and make amends if needed. Guilt can drag you down and cause you to lose.

Don't be too concerned about what the world thinks of you, and center your life around your family and friends. Don't keep a running score or compare yourself to others. If your life does not turn out the way you have envisioned, join the crowd and be thankful for what you have. Your focus should not be on you but on those who depend on you for survival. Gallon and Gardner put up amazing personal numbers, but they always had the best interests of the team at heart.

Do your job and give back to your community and your loved ones. You can accomplish wonderful individual things, but make your team's accomplishments the priority. Life is not about you but what you can do for those around you. Go Blue!

List the ways you are dependable.

THE CATCH

Cyle Young

September 14, 1991: Notre Dame at Michigan

THE 1991 MEETING BETWEEN THE Notre Dame
Fighting Irish and the University of Michigan Wolverines
was precipitated by four straight Notre Dame victories.
The Lou Holtz–coached Irish team was always a force
to be reckoned with. In recent seasons, Notre Dame had
won a national championship, been undefeated, and had
a Heisman Trophy winner. The 1991 team arriving in Ann
Arbor for Michigan's first home game of the season would
not roll over easily.

Michigan entered the game as the number four team
in the country, and Notre Dame rolled in with a number
six ranking. The following week, the Wolverines would
also host the number one Florida State Seminoles, but
they couldn't overlook the dangerous Fighting Irish. The
matchup of top five teams would be broadcast across the
nation, and the game would be one for the ages.

Coming into the game, Michigan was led by quarterback Elvis Grbac, who had played at St. Joseph High School
in Cleveland, Ohio, with current teammate wide receiver

Desmond Howard. The Notre Dame squad included full-back Jerome Bettis, a future NFL Hall of Fame player. In a recruiting coup, Bettis, the state of Michigan's top 1989 high school football player and Gatorade Player of the Year, decided to join Notre Dame over one of the in-state programs. But even though Notre Dame had bested Michigan for a great player like Jerome Bettis, victories weren't won solely on the recruiting trail—they had to be won on the field.

By halftime, Michigan had tucked the lead away 17–7. Grbac put up an impressive display of accuracy, going 20–22 over the course of the game. It seemed like he just couldn't miss.

A 10-point halftime lead wasn't enough to stop Notre Dame from coming back to make it a difficult contest. In the third quarter, the Fighting Irish's Rick Mirer threw a 35-yard touchdown pass to wide receiver Tony Smith. The score brought Notre Dame to within 3 points, 17–14, at the end of the quarter. It was still anyone's game. The televised matchup was living up to all the hype.

Early in the fourth quarter, Grbac drove the Wolverine offense down the field. The Irish defense held on their own 25-yard line, forcing Michigan to either kick a field goal or go for it on fourth-and-one. The field goal wouldn't secure enough of a lead to protect the score from being overtaken by a Notre Dame touchdown, so Michigan's head coach, Gary Moeller, decided to go for it.

On fourth-and-one, Moeller called in the play, but as Grbac surveyed the defense, he thought the play wouldn't work. He called a time-out to discuss the coverage with his head coach, who called the same play. Grbac strut-ted back on the field and, as the defense adjusted their coverage to the Wolverine formation, realized the play should work this time.

The Wolverines snapped the ball, and Grbac dropped back. He pump-faked once. The defensive end jumped on the fake, and the corner bit. He hesitated momentarily in his coverage, and Desmond Howard juked and raced behind him.

The quarterback thought he'd overthrown his receiver. "When it left my hand it was kind of wobbly. It was really high," Grbac said after the game. "Des was running as hard as he could, and the ball was just floating."

But Grbac didn't overthrow Howard. The ball hung in the air, floating into the back corner of the end zone. And like magic, Howard reached out for the ball. He jumped forward, with arms extended. As he stretched, his body seemed to float in the air, but he caught the ball.

The crowd erupted, and a national television audience was treated to one of the most spectacular catches ever recorded. The famous catch earned Desmond Howard the nickname Magic and continues to live on in multiple replays on the internet and during every Michigan football season. Howard's performance vaulted him onto the Heisman Trophy radar as one of the best players in the country. He became a household name as the 1991 Wolverines managed to pull together a top-six season. Howard's 905 receiving yards and nineteen touchdowns were impressive, but when you added on his two rushing touchdowns and his two kickoff and punt return touchdowns, he was a force to be reckoned with every time he touched the football. Not bad for a five foot eleven receiver from Ohio.

Michigan would go on to win the game, but it's the catch that everyone remembers. The amazing play never would have happened if Coach Gary Moeller had second-guessed himself. He stuck to his guns. Moeller knew what play he wanted to call, and he knew he had the personnel to pull it off. After the game, when the coach was asked about that specific play, he said, "When it works, it takes a guy like Elvis to throw it, a guy like Desmond to make it work and make me look smart."

And smart is exactly how that play call made him look.

STICK TO YOUR PLAY CALL

It's hard to stick to your play call or game plan when you feel that your adversary has your number. That kind of tenacity requires a type of confidence that not many possess. Have you ever had moments in your life when you changed your direction or plan because of the pressure of a situation or relationship? If so, how did it work out? Do you wish you could go back and stick to your original plan?

STAY THE COURSE

Staying your course can be difficult when outside influences pressure you to change your path or modify your destination. Make a commitment to have courage and resist outside temptations and influences. Wake up every day and reaffirm your goal. Rise and restate—write your goals down if you need to and recite them the first thing each morning. The more you are convinced of your objectives, the harder it will be for you to be pulled off course. Protect your goals and limit your contact with negative people who don't affirm you and the plans you have for your life, relationships, work, or education. Go Blue!

How do you think you can be more consistent in the future when it comes to knowing what you want to accomplish and not veering from your course due to outside pressures or influences?

_____

_____

_____

_____

_____

_____

_____

_____

_____

_____

_____

_____

_____

_____

_____

_____

_____

_____

_____

_____

_____

_____

_____

_____

_____

_____

_____

BE ACCOUNTABLE TO
YOUR TEAM

Del Duduit

November 21, 1964: Michigan 10, Ohio State 0

THE UNIVERSITY OF MICHIGAN HAD not won at the
Horseshoe in Columbus since 1956. But today would be
different as the Wolverines flexed their defensive muscles
and shut out the Ohio State University Buckeyes 10–0.
With the win, the Maize and Blue earned a trip to the
prestigious Rose Bowl. To add icing to the cake, the win
spoiled Ohio State's plans to travel to Pasadena, California, and squashed any hopes of a coveted conference
title.

The Michigan defense forced six Buckeye fumbles,
one of which came in the second quarter and led to the
Wolverines' lone touchdown. The score came when Ohio
State punt returner Bob Rein muffed the catch, and Michigan recovered with just under a minute left in the half.
Moments later, Wolverine quarterback Bob Timberlake
found Jim Detwiler for the 17-yard touchdown. Timberlake, who was from the Columbus area, booted the extra
point through the uprights for the 7–0 lead.

Early in the final quarter, Timberlake gave the Wolverines some cushion when he nailed a 27-yard field goal and a 10–0 advantage. Ohio State coach Woody Hayes admitted after the game that his Buckeyes were outplayed by Michigan. Timberlake accounted for all the 10 points needed to knock off the rival Ohio State Buckeyes. He led the Wolverines to their first Big Ten Conference title since 1950. He did it all on the offense the entire season. He threw for 807 yards and ran for 574 yards, which was enormous production for a quarterback in those days. The offense outscored their opponents 235 to 83, and the team finished with a record of 8–1. He also led Michigan to a 34–7 win over the Oregon State Beavers to claim the Rose Bowl championship.

Timberlake was chosen as a first team All-American in 1964 and was awarded the Chicago Tribune Silver Football trophy, given to the conference's most valuable player. Over his three-year stint at Michigan, he gained 315 yards on the ground and 1,507 in the air. He had nineteen touchdowns and was the team's punter and kicker, scoring 36 extra points and 18 points in field goals. In all, he was responsible for 121 points.

He was accountable to his team. Are you? You might have goals, either personal or professional. How do you ensure you reach them? What steps do you take to be responsible?

EXAMINE THE PLAYBOOK

Life is full of third-and-eight opportunities. Nothing of any worth comes easily, and you shouldn't want it to anyway. You should strive to work and earn your recognition.

There are times when the easy road might present itself, and you should never pass that up. But for the most part, a win takes effort and dedication. Perhaps your goal is to retire at age fifty. Maybe you want to be the boss or even a vice president of your company. Those are wonderful and admirable goals. But at what cost will you earn the recognition? What will you sacrifice? Your time? Your family?

EXECUTE THE PLAY

First you must figure out the most important aspects of your life and look for ways to improve. Come up with a mission statement of your own, and form a personal board of directors. Meet with these colleagues once a month over coffee, without distractions, and give and receive honest feedback. Let them hold you accountable for your personal goals. If you are doing something that might cause a negative reputation, then adhere to their advice. Nothing is worth trashing your name. Be open to feedback, and never get upset when you hear something you don't like about yourself.

Stay on top of your to-do lists. Once you get behind, it may be difficult to climb back to the top. Be aware of your strengths and weaknesses. Never be afraid to ask questions or get help. Stay humble and own up to your mistakes. Never throw anyone under the bus, and take responsibility for your wins and losses. Be sure to manage your time and prioritize your obligations. The best thing to remember is to laugh often, especially at yourself. Timberlake was accountable to his team and led them to

success on the field. You have an obligation to make sure
your family finishes first in your conference. Go Blue!

What are your top priorities?

_____

_____

_____

_____

_____

_____

_____

_____

_____

_____

_____

_____

_____

_____

_____

_____

_____

_____

_____

_____

_____

_____

_____

_____

_____

_____

NIGHT GAME

Cyle Young

August 20, 2011: Notre Dame at Michigan

THE 2011 MEETING BETWEEN UNIVERSITY of Notre Dame and University of Michigan took place during the first ever night game at Michigan Stadium. A primetime viewing audience would be treated to a fantastic and exciting game that would go down to the wire for the first ever Under the Lights.

Notre Dame entered the game 0–1 in the season. In Coach Brian Kelly's second season in South Bend, the team had struggled to find their rhythm, losing a close game to number sixteen ranked South Florida, 20–23. The game against the 1–0 Wolverines would provide the opportunity to right the ship and get the Fighting Irish's 2011 season back on track.

But the Wolverines were led by electric playmaker quarterback Denard "Shoelace" Robinson. With Robinson on the field, the Wolverines were always in the game.

The matchup brought another record crowd to Michigan Stadium: 114,804 would witness one of the greatest comebacks in Michigan football history.

Notre Dame stormed out to a 17–7 lead. Irish quarterback Tommy Rees connected over and over again with his wide receiver Michael Floyd. Rees would finish the game with twenty-seven completions for 315 yards, and Floyd would haul in an astounding thirteen receptions for 159 yards.

At halftime, the Irish were well in control of the game and looked like they would go on to beat the Wolverines by an impressive margin. The third quarter continued in the same fashion, and Notre Dame controlled both the time of possession and the scoreboard.

But late in the third quarter, Robinson led his team down the field. As the quarter ended, Robinson had positioned his team deep into Notre Dame territory—the 1-yard line.

The fourth quarter opened with Robinson plunging forward for a 1-yard touchdown, bringing the Wolverines to within 10 points, 24–14. The Wolverine defense held the Irish to a three-and-out and forced a punt—which fell short, and the Wolverines would take over possession on a short field, starting at the Notre Dame 40-yard line. Five plays later Robinson hit receiver Jeremy Gallon for a 14-yard touchdown to close the lead to three points.

Notre Dame responded to the Wolverines' two scores with an extended drive of their own. Seven plays and 4:39 later, the Fighting Irish had a first-and-goal on the Michigan 7-yard line. But the Wolverine defense forced Irish quarterback Rees to fumble, and Michigan recovered the ball on the 9-yard line.

Michigan couldn't convert the opportunity into more points because Robinson was intercepted as the team drove into Irish territory. Thankfully, the Michigan defense once again forced the Irish to a quick punt. With 2:05 left in the game, the fast-striking Michigan offense charged down the field in five plays to score a touchdown and take the lead for the first time in the game, 28–24.

But Notre Dame wasn't finished yet. A decent kickoff return and a pass interference penalty by the Wolverines gave the Irish a short field. Notre Dame capitalized on the field position, and Rees tossed a 29-yard touchdown pass to Theo Riddick. You could almost hear every Wolverine fan sigh at the same time. With only twenty-eight seconds left, Michigan had fallen behind 31–28.

Michigan still had "Shoelace." They couldn't be counted out. Robinson's first pass fell incomplete, but his second attempt was a 64-yard strike to Jeremy Gallon. Michigan had first-and-ten at the Notre Dame 16 with eight seconds remaining in the game.

On the next play, Robinson found Roy Roundtree for the go-ahead score, 35–31. With only two seconds left, Notre Dame wouldn't have any miracles left, and Michigan completed one of its greatest comebacks ever.

No matter how difficult the trial, Michigan believed they could come from behind and still win the game. There were only a few ticks left on the clock, and they believed that with Robinson leading the team, that's all the time they would need. Not many teams in the history of college football could ever say that with the same level of confidence, but they didn't have "Shoelace."

Do you have that same level of confidence in yourself? Do you believe that you can overcome all odds even if you have only a few moments left to do it?

EXUDE CONFIDENCE

The 2011 Michigan team believed, and you can, too. Have faith in yourself. You are capable of doing amazing things, but it all starts with believing in your ability and preparation. Don't listen to outsiders. Not many people believed the 2011 Wolverines were going to make a 17-point fourth-quarter comeback. And even when they did, those same people thought that the Irish's final touchdown had sealed a Notre Dame victory. But history has revealed the inaccuracy of those types of thoughts. Michigan won, even when it wasn't likely, and even when naysayers thought otherwise. The only thing that matters in your life is what you know to be true about yourself and what you know that you can accomplish. Go out and prove your doubters wrong!

GO OUT AND DO IT

Don't buy into the negativity of your detractors. You can flip the script on them and use their cynicism as fuel to propel you forward toward your goals. Impassioned by your newfound desire, work harder, think smarter, make better decisions and press onward in the face of any doubter. Resist the urge to be too arrogant to listen to others advice and seek wise council. Educate yourself on how others have had similar successes in life, work, relationships and then go out and achieve those same successes for yourself. You can do many amazing things if you accept advice, work hard, and put your whole heart into your goals. Go Blue!

What are some amazing things you've already accomplished even though others didn't believe in you? Is there anything holding you back from doing something awesome?

_____
_____
_____
_____
_____
_____
_____
_____
_____
_____
_____
_____
_____
_____
_____
_____
_____
_____
_____
_____
_____
_____
_____
_____
_____
_____
_____

DON'T BE A GLORY HOG

Del Duduit

October 26, 1985: Michigan 42, Indiana 15

THERE IS A REASON THE fans at University of Michigan have strong affection for Jim Harbaugh as a coach and a player. The fiery quarterback from Toledo, Ohio, enjoyed a remarkable career. He finished as Michigan's all-time record holder with 5,449 yards passing. At the time he played, he was second on the all-time list with 620 passing attempts, resulting in 387 completions (62.4 percent) and thirty-one touchdowns. He held the NCAA D-I record for passing efficiency at 149.6 for more than ten years.

But his true Maize and Blue colors were on brilliant display on October 26, 1985. It was homecoming at the Big House, and more than 105,600 fans crammed into the stadium to watch the Big Ten matchup with the visiting Hoosiers of Indiana University. The crowd was a bit restless during the first two quarters. Indiana took a 9–7 lead at the end of the first period but shared a 15–15 tie at the intermission. Adjustments were made in the locker room, and Michigan outscored the Hoosiers 27–0 in the second half.

Harbaugh played at a high level. He completed seventeen of twenty-three attempts for 283 yards and two touchdowns. His effort broke the school's single-game record of 259 yards set the previous year by Chris Zurbrugg. He hit all his favorite receivers. Eric Kattus hauled in five catches for 123 yards, and Paul Jokisch caught four passes for 91 yards. On the ground, running back Jamie Morris earned 179 yards and two scores.

But this was Harbaugh's day. He was brilliant. After the game, he was asked how it felt to break the school passing mark. "Records are nice, but everything we do here is team oriented. Everyone's telling me about the record, but they should tell it to Paul Jokisch and Eric Kattus and John Kolesar. They caught the passes," he said.

He put the team ahead of himself. He knew that without the others on the squad, he could not have accomplished anything. There would have not been a win without the other players.

In the final three games of the season, he continued his hot hand. Harbaugh completed forty-one of fifty passes for 706 yards and nine touchdowns, and he did not throw any interceptions. Fans in Michigan appreciated his efforts as a player, but they truly admired the way he put the team ahead of himself.

In a sport where a lot of attention goes to a few players, it's refreshing when a leader gives credit to those around him and lifts them up in public.

What about you? Do you make sure your teammates at work or at home get the recognition they deserve? You might receive some of the limelight, but could you reach your goals without help from those around you?

GIVE CREDIT WHERE IT BELONGS

Harbaugh put up impressive numbers in the game against Indiana. But ten other players on offense contributed to his success. He had linemen who gave protection and running backs who drew attention from other defenders. And his receivers ran good routes and caught the passes. But since he played the high-profile position, he received the accolades.

Perhaps you are in a similar situation at work. You might be on a team that has made significant strides to aid in your company's success. One person receives the credit for what many achieved—this happens often in the corporate world. But do you let everyone else know that your accomplishments are a result of everyone around you? It's easy to shake hands and take bonus checks and promotions, but do you acknowledge those around you who also sacrificed? What about your family and all those missed practices or school plays? Success has a price, and if you reach that goal, do you take in all the glory for yourself?

BE A TEAM PLAYER

Harbaugh demonstrated why he is the ultimate team player. Although his name appeared as the record holder, he made sure others were acknowledged publicly. You can take the same approach. There is nothing wrong with success until it brings selfishness. Recognize your own tendency to focus all the attention on yourself. When you realize and recognize you have had help along the way, you can elevate others.

For instance, you went through training, and your supervisors coached you along the way. Your family showed support and encouragement. Your success is also theirs. Always give others glory and honor before you take it for yourself. Give the people in your professional and personal lives the roses they deserve for putting up with you. Then, the best thing you can do is reach out and help someone else attain their goals. You needed help and received it. Now it's your turn to encourage others. Go Blue!

List three people who have helped you along the way.

_____

_____

_____

_____

_____

_____

_____

_____

_____

_____

_____

_____

_____

_____

_____

_____

_____

_____

_____

BADGER BATTLE

Cyle Young

September 27, 2008: Wisconsin at Michigan

RICH RODRIGUEZ'S FIRST SEASON AT University of Michigan was an overwhelming disappointment. For the first time in 129 years of Michigan football, the team had recorded nine losses in a single season. The installation of Rodriguez's spread option offense was ill matched for Michigan's current football personnel.

But in a season of devastating losses to the usual conference cupcakes—Northwestern University, Purdue University, University of Illinois, and Mid-American Conference opponent University of Toledo—Michigan managed to create one bright spot.

The University of Wisconsin Badgers came rolling into Ann Arbor with a number nine ranking and high aspirations of a championship-caliber season. Michigan had struggled through the first three games, posting a 1–2 record. Wisconsin started the season undefeated, and their stop in Ann Arbor was supposed to be another easy victory that would help tune them up for a big-time matchup the following week with high-ranked Ohio State.

Everything seemed to point to this outcome at half-time. Wisconsin left the field with a 19–0 lead. They'd held the Wolverines to just one first down, five turnovers, and just 21 yards in the entire first half. But that abysmal offensive performance fired the Wolverines up at half-time. Wolverine senior nose tackle Terrance Taylor made an impassioned speech, imploring his teammates to get their acts together and get their heads in the game. They could win, he said, if they pulled together.

The group of players that entered the field in the second half played like an entirely different team. Michigan would gain twelve times as many yards in the second half—247 yards. The defense held strong against the Badger offense, and the Wolverines managed to get on the scoreboard in the third quarter when Michigan quarterback Steven Threet found tight end Kevin Koger for a 26-yard touchdown.

With 10:27 left in the game, Michigan scored again on a 34-yard Brandon Minor touchdown run, bringing the game to 19–14. On the very next play, Michigan linebacker Josh Thompson scored on a pick-six interception return for a touchdown. The Wolverines failed a 2-point conversion but still managed to take over the lead, 20–19.

The game's momentum had swung wildly into the Wolverines' favor. Wisconsin couldn't turn their next drive into any points, and five minutes later, Wolverine running back Sam McGuffie scored a 3-yard touchdown, putting the game firmly in Michigan's control, 27–19.

But the Badgers weren't done scoring. They methodically moved the ball down the field using their two-minute offense. With thirteen seconds left in the game, Badger receiver Allan Evridge hauled in a 22-yard touchdown pass to bring Wisconsin to within 2 points. A successful 2-point attempt would send the game to overtime.

Wisconsin converted the 2-point attempt, but it was called back on a penalty—ineligible receiver downfield. Michigan's defense prevented the second attempt and recovered the ensuing onside kick to preserve the victory.

Earlier in the game, it hadn't seemed likely that the Wolverines could defeat Wisconsin, but they did. They buckled their chinstraps after halftime and went back on the field to play football. They could have wallowed in self-pity and just let the Badgers continue to score touchdowns in Michigan Stadium, but they refused to go down without a fight—and they ended up with the win.

FASTEN YOUR CHINSTRAP

No matter how bad it seems to get, you just keep fighting. Push forward and carve out your own success. We all experience dark times in life, times when everything seems to be going the wrong way and we don't seem to be headed in the right direction. The 2008 Wolverines were no stranger to that feeling, but even in times of despair, they still managed to pull together and create moments of great success.

Don't let the atmosphere around you define you. Just because everything seems wrong and out of place, you don't have to give up. Buckle your chinstrap and get back in the game. You might not have someone to give you a Terrance Taylor–style motivational speech to get you pumped up, but get back in the game anyway.

You can have that come-from-behind success, too. Don't give up.

NEVER LISTEN TO THE ODDS

Some of the world's most famous people have overcome great odds before having success. Albert Einstein didn't spoke until he was four years old. Jim Carrey experienced homelessness as a child. Bill Gates's first business failed, and Stephen King's first novel was rejected thirty times. Don't let the odds define you.

Avoid the comparison trap. You don't have to be like anyone else, and you don't have to achieve your success in the same way or on the same timetable as someone else. If you want to create your own come-from-behind victory, it first starts with believing in yourself. Turn a deaf ear to critics and follow your plan to success and victory. Go Blue!

What was your biggest come-from-behind victory? How did you find the strength to rally yourself and go for the win?

DEFEND YOUR HOUSE

Del Duduit

September 27, 2008: Michigan 27, Wisconsin 25

IT WAS THE FIVE HUNDREDTH game at the Big House. The unranked Wolverines hosted number nine University of Wisconsin, and things didn't look good at halftime for the Michigan faithful. The Maize and Blue had only 21 yards and committed five turnovers. It was no wonder they trailed 19–0 at the intermission.

It seemed like déjà vu because they'd had six turnovers the week before in a loss to Notre Dame. Players could have easily given up hope for a comeback. The easy approach would have been to toss the towel in the air and go home.

On the second possession of the half, Michigan quarterback Steven Threet connected with Kevin Koger for a 26-yard touchdown to culminate an 80-yard drive. That was a big confidence booster for Threet, since he went two of ten for negative 7 yards in the first half. He finished the game twelve of thirty-one with 96 yards passing and 89 yards rushing. He was a different player in the second half.

Early in the fourth quarter, running back Brandon Minor romped for a 34-yard touchdown, and the Wolverines were closer. They added four field goals to get to 27, and the Michigan defense did the rest, holding the Badgers at bay in the second half. Brandon Graham was among the leaders on defense as he sacked Wisconsin quarterback Allan Evridge three times and forced two fumbles. Wisconsin managed to score with thirteen seconds to play in the game. A penalty on a successful 2-point conversion led to an incomplete pass, and Michigan won the game.

The offense may have received the glory and headlines, but the defense was the reason the team was able to come back and win. After the game, Threet was asked about the astonishing comeback, but he hesitated to take credit. Instead, he praised and talked about how tremendously the defense played and said the team never would have had the chance to win if not for them.

Graham was determined to help his team win with a solid defensive performance. After the season, he was recognized as a second-team All-Big Ten Conference selection and earned the team MVP award for the Wolverines.

Defense can win the battle for field position, and it can halt an opponent's offensive threat. A swarming defense can force turnovers and throw an offense out of sync.

Have you ever had to use defense mechanisms of your own?

LINE UP THE DEFENSE

Have you ever been the victim of a lie or had your reputation smeared? It's not uncommon. Unfortunately, people tend to believe an untruth when it is juicy or torrid. They often take pleasure when someone else takes a fall and looks bad in the eyes of the world.

A reputation takes a long time to build up, but it can be taken down within days. You may have never intended for something to happen, but it has. Perhaps you were seen having lunch with a person of the opposite sex. The meeting may have been platonic, but someone who saw it thought otherwise. Or maybe you are friends on social media with a person who has an awful reputation. Observers may view this as guilt by association and think you share the same ideas.

GO ON OFFENSE

Your name is valuable to you and your family and friends. There are ways to take precautions against unwarranted attacks. To avoid the big loss, be proactive and conduct a Google search of your name once a month. Then establish a Google alert for your name to let you know if your identity has appeared online. Do the same for some people you follow.

Never allow anyone to tag you in a post with pictures if you do not know them. And always think a few seconds before you hit the "send" button. If you have any doubts or apprehensions, delete the post. You hear of news accounts where something someone posted three years ago has come back to haunt them. Your social media footprint will be around forever, and what you do online can have consequences.

Be careful about whom you follow and who follows you. There are many traps out there waiting for someone to step into them. When you think it might be private and for your eyes only, then think twice. You have one reputation, and you must always be on the defense. Never be caught off guard and have your name smeared on social media.

Graham knew the importance of stopping Wisconsin's offense if the Wolverines were to make a comeback. He did his job and protected his Big House and gave the offense the opportunity to score. You must do the same thing. Watch your back, and be a positive force in your community and family. Your reputation is at stake. Go Blue!

How can you improve your image?

_____

_____

_____

_____

_____

_____

_____

_____

_____

_____

_____

_____

_____

_____

_____

_____

_____

_____

ORANGE BOWL

Cyle Young

January 1, 2000: Alabama vs. Michigan

THE UNIVERSITY OF MICHIGAN RECEIVED an at-large bid to play in the Orange Bowl against Southeastern Conference (SEC) champion University of Alabama. Two midseason upset losses had derailed the Wolverines' Big Ten Championship season, but four straight wins over ranked opponents to finish the season raised Michigan to a number five ranking.

Alabama, similarly, had suffered two early season defeats, but a win in the SEC Championship game propelled them onward to the Orange Bowl. Running back Shaun Alexander led the potent Alabama offense. Alexander, a Kentucky native, had chosen to attend Alabama over Michigan during the 1995 recruiting cycle. Early in the season, the powerful back had been a leading Heisman Trophy candidate, but an injured knee dropped him in the final rankings. But by January 1, Alexander's knee was back to full health. He propelled his team to a 14–0 lead midway through the second quarter.

Michigan struggled to find a running game against the staunch Alabama defensive line, rushing for only 27 yards on twenty-three attempts in the game. Alabama looked to be cruising to any easy win until Wolverine quarterback Tom Brady found wide receiver David Terrell for a 27-yard touchdown pass. The team would close out the half down 7 points.

The Wolverines received the third-quarter kickoff. Terrell and Brady connected on another long touchdown pass, this time for 57 yards. Michigan's passing offense showed signs of life.

But Alabama wasn't going to sit back and give the game away. Alexander erupted through the Michigan defense on the next drive for a 50-yard touchdown run. On Michigan's next offensive possession, they punted to the dangerous punt returner Freddie Milons, who frustrated the Wolverines' punt coverage, going 62 yards for a punt-return touchdown and moving the lead to 14 points.

Midway through the third quarter, Michigan found themselves in a position similar to where they had been in the second quarter. They would overcome the deficit the same way, on a 20-yard touchdown pass from Brady to Terrell. Michigan running back Anthony Thomas would punch in a 1-yard touchdown on the team's final drive of the third quarter to tie the game 28–28. Twice Michigan had stormed back from 14-point deficits.

Both teams' defenses held in the fourth quarter, sending the game to overtime. Michigan had multiple chances to win in the fourth, but a goal-line fumble by running back Thomas and a blocked Hayden Epstein field goal would send the game into overtime.

Alabama won the coin toss and chose to give Michigan the first overtime possession. On the first play of overtime, Brady found tight end Shawn Thompson for a 25-yard touchdown. Kicker Epstein converted the extra point.

The Crimson Tide would need only two plays to get in the end zone. After a 4-yard run by Alexander, Alabama quarterback Andrew Zow tossed a 21-yard touchdown to Antonio Carter. The game ended when Alabama kicker Ryan Pflugner pushed the extra point wide right. Michigan won its first ever overtime bowl game 35–34.

The 2000 Orange Bowl created the legend of Tom Brady. At an Orange Bowl ring ceremony in Ann Arbor fifteen years later, Brady penned a letter to his teammates. In it he shared that the comeback against Alabama in the Orange Bowl had set the tone for his entire career. When he was faced with a deficit in his first ever Super Bowl with the New England Patriots, Brady said, the confidence he had gained in the overtime comeback in Florida gave him the confidence that he could come back and win the biggest game in the NFL season. The Patriots would go on to win the game.

Have you ever experienced a great comeback? How were you able to take a difficult situation and turn it around?

FASTEN YOUR CHINSTRAP

Michigan looked to be on the ropes twice in the game against Alabama. Without a successful running attack, Michigan could have easily given up. But quarterback

Tom Brady wasn't going to go down without a fight. He was going to will his team to victory, even if he had to shoulder much of the burden himself. Brady finished the game thirty-four of forty-six for 369 yards and four touchdowns.

The cocaptain and team leader didn't quit on his team. You don't have to quit on your team, your coworkers, or your family either. Life will go sideways from time to time. When you feel like the momentum has shifted away from you, don't give up. Grit your teeth and get ready to make a miraculous comeback. But don't be alarmed if, like the Wolverines, you come back only to find yourself immediately down and out again. Make another comeback, and this time go on to have the personal victory or success you desire.

When, on multiple occasions, you are able to pull yourself and your spirit together and charge back against adversity, it defines you. That kind of effort shapes and changes you, and it will mold your future.

CALL IT A COMEBACK

When scaling a tough mountain in your life, you must first get in the proper mindset to overcome adversity. You've got to drop any negative self-talk and begin having self-compassion. You will never scale the mountains in your life by doubting or diminishing yourself. Change your response to difficult situations and have compassion on your own limits, mistakes, and setbacks. When you discontinue allowing yourself to be limited by self-loathing, you move from a victim mentality to taking full possession and responsibility of your life. Embracing full responsibility with a positive outlook can help you follow the game plan and make the climb all the way to the top. Go Blue!

When was the last time you faced an uphill battle? How were you able to pull ahead and scale the mountain?

_____

_____

_____

_____

_____

_____

_____

_____

_____

_____

_____

_____

_____

_____

_____

_____

_____

_____

_____

_____

_____

_____

_____

_____

_____

WEEK 39

—ᜈᜈ—

BE UNSTOPPABLE

Del Duduit

September 28, 1940: Michigan 41, California 0

THE FIRST GAME OF THE 1940 season set the tone for what would be a good year for the University of Michigan. Running back Tom Harmon had a day most athletes only dream about. It was his twenty-first birthday, and he celebrated the occasion in style. The senior from Rensselaer, Indiana, scored four touchdowns and kicked four extra points. He even threw a touchdown pass for good measure. He made a bold statement when he returned the opening kickoff 94 yards for a score. This set the tone that it was going to be a good day for the birthday boy.

In the second quarter, he returned a punt 72 yards for another touchdown. Game reports stated he dashed from side to side in a dazzling run and ran about 115 yards before he crossed the goal line.

He later added an 85-yard run before halftime and dodged a fan who came onto the field to try to help California stop him. Newspaper reports described Harmon as a "greased pig" and noted the defense was "a wet paper bag." Michigan coach Fritz Crisler hailed Harmon as the greatest player he had ever coached. Harmon enjoyed a successful and productive career at the Maize and Blue. A few of his accolades included:

- The Maxwell Award in 1940, given to the nation's best football player
- The Heisman Trophy in 1940, awarded to the most outstanding player
- Associated Press Athlete of the Year in 1940
- The Big Ten MVP in 1940
- First Team All-American
- All-Big Ten Team
- Michigan Sports Hall of Fame

In his three years as a Wolverine, he rushed for 2,151 yards on 399 carries. He completed 101 of 233 passes for 1,369 yards and had sixteen touchdowns. He scored a total of thirty-three touchdowns, which broke Red Grange's record of thirty-one scores. Toward the end of the 1940s, his number, ninety-eight, was retired, but in 2013 the school unretired the number as part of the Michigan's Football Legends program. Devin Gardner was selected to be the first player to wear the jersey since 1940.

After college, Harmon went on to serve in the military and was assigned to the 449th Fighter-Interceptor Squadron in China in 1943. On one of his missions, his plane was shot down by a Japanese Zero in a dogfight. He reportedly took down two Japanese planes. He was forced to bail out of his plane into China and was later rescued by anti-Japanese Chinese guerillas. He was awarded the Purple Heart and the Silver Star. His story was published under the title *Pilots Also Pray* in 1944. He was discharged as a captain when World War II ended in 1945.

Harmon returned to the States and played professional football with the Green Bay Packers. He married actress Elyse Knox and had three children: Kristin Harmon, who married singer Rick Nelson; Kelly Harmon, who was a model and later married the publisher of *Sports Illustrated*; and Mark Harmon, who is an accomplished actor.

He gave 100 percent when he played on the field and in the military. He never backed down and lived a full life.

How do you perform? Do you shine at work and at home? How valuable are you? Do you excel?

WATCH THE GAME FILM

You don't have to be number one in everything you do. But you do need to give life your best effort. Your family deserves nothing less than 100 percent from you. So does your employer, and if you own your business, then your survival depends on your efforts. Life is not meant to be observed from the sidelines. Get in the game and make an impact on your friends and loved ones.

COME OUT OF THE TUNNEL

Success in life is not measured in MVP awards or trophies. These are nice, and there is nothing wrong with recognition. But you want mostly to be remembered for being a person of integrity. If you have little ones to raise, if you volunteer as a Big Brother/Big Sister, or you have any other regular contact with kids and young adults, you want to set a positive example. Instead of making a 94-yard kickoff return, do the little things that add up to something big. Keep your word and be on time. Take responsibility for your actions and stay focused on doing good. Show respect to your family and those in authority, and never judge anyone. Stay humble and grateful and remember to laugh often, especially at yourself.

These attributes will get you enshrined into your family's Hall of Fame. You may not have played for a powerhouse like Michigan, parachuted behind enemy lines, or married a movie star, but you can make a big difference. Live your life, and make those around you happy and proud. Go Blue!

How can you make those around you smile more?

_____

_____

_____

_____

_____

_____

_____

_____

_____

_____

_____

_____

_____

_____

_____

_____

_____

_____

_____

_____

_____

_____

WINTER PREPARATION

—ᴍᴍ—

LITTLE BROWN JUG

Cyle Young

October 10, 2003: Wisconsin at Michigan

IN 2003, MICHIGAN PLAYED ITS one hundredth game against the University of Minnesota. The Wolverines entered the rivalry game having won fourteen straight against the Golden Gophers. The victor of the game would take home one of college football's oldest trophies, the Little Brown Jug.

After going 6–0 to start the season, Minnesota had climbed to a number seventeen ranking—a rare feat for the Golden Gophers. The Wolverines had lost two earlier contests and stumbled into Minneapolis with a number twenty ranking. For the first time in many years, Minnesota was favored over the Wolverines—and they were ready to reclaim the Little Brown Jug.

Minnesota dominated the first half and went into halftime with a 14–0 lead. At the start of the fourth quarter, Michigan trailed 28–7. The Golden Gopher running attack bruised the Michigan defense, and the final quarter looked to be just another opportunity for Minnesota to pad their rushing stats.

On the Wolverines' first possession in the fourth quarter, quarterback John Navarre led the team 80 yards on ten plays. He accented the drive with a 10-yard touchdown pass to running back Chris Perry.

Michigan defender Jacob Stewart intercepted Minnesota quarterback Asad Abdul-Kahliq's pass and returned it for a 35-yard touchdown, to bring the score to 21–28. Abdul-Khaliq wouldn't let that score stand for long. On Minnesota's next drive, he split through the Wolverine defense and raced 52 yards for another Golden Gopher touchdown. The score was now 35–21.

The Wolverines would equal that score with a short drive of their own. John Navarre found receiver Braylon Edwards for a 52-yard Michigan touchdown. The Wolverines were still down, but they weren't yet out of the game.

Michigan held. The defense forced Minnesota to only four plays. Wolverine running back Chris Perry had two receptions and two rushes on the next 60-yard offensive drive. His second rush attempt sent him 10 yards for the tying touchdown, bringing the score to 35–35.

Another three-and-out gave Michigan the ball and another short field. They capitalized on a twelve-play 42-yard drive with a go-ahead field goal. They pulled ahead, 38–35.

But Minnesota still had time on the clock. The Gophers pushed down the field, but a Marcus Curry interception sealed the game for the Wolverines—giving the team its greatest come-from-behind victory in the history of Michigan football. The Wolverines scored 31 points in the fourth quarter to take home the Little Brown Jug and extend their streak of victories over Minnesota to fifteen.

Scoring 31 points in the fourth quarter is a difficult task for any team. In the National Football League, only four teams have ever scored 31 points or more in the fourth quarter, and only one team in the last twenty years. Michigan managed to pull off the impressive feat not only in the fourth quarter but also in an effort to come from behind *and* win the game. The comeback won't often be repeated and will live on as one of Michigan's greatest games.

The victory against Minnesota righted the listing ship of Michigan's season. Two losses in three games had dropped the team from number three in the country to number twenty. Another loss would knock them out of the top twenty-five and virtually end their season. But the miracle comeback sparked the Wolverines. Something seemed to click for the 2003 team from that point on. Over the course of the next five games, they climbed back into the national spotlight and up to a number four ranking. A victory over Ohio State sent the Wolverines to the Rose Bowl against USC.

NEVER QUIT

Like Michigan, you can also experience a come-from-behind victory. Not every great accomplishment in life is attained by being in the lead. Many times, you'll have to dig deep and find yourself when the going gets tough. If you find yourself behind your competition, don't get down on yourself. You can still achieve all that you desire, but you will have to overcome a disadvantage or competitive position.

Have you ever found yourself having to come-from-behind? How did you feel?

COME FROM BEHIND

You can achieve your own miraculous win, even if others have counted you out. Spend some time learning about some of the world's most famous athletes, artists, and inventors. Many of them were counted out by naysayers, but they overcame with tenacity and an industrious passion, and you can too. You have to dig deep. Put in more hours. Ask for more advice and counsel. You have to give every effort toward realizing your goals. Only then will you achieve against all odds and carve out an unexpected win. Go Blue!

What was your greatest come-from-behind victory? Did it inspire you to go on and do great things?

_____

_____

_____

_____

_____

_____

_____

_____

_____

_____

_____

_____

_____

_____

_____

_____

LET YOUR REPUTATION
SPEAK FOR ITSELF

Del Duduit

January 1, 1965: Michigan 34, Oregon State 7

THE NUMBER FOUR RANKED WOLVERINES marched
into the Rose Bowl in Pasadena and faced the Oregon
State Beavers on New Year's Day in 1965. Michigan was
an 11-point favorite for a reason. The team's leader was
Robert Timberlake, and the bigger-than-life quarterback
did it all. He passed, ran, kicked, and motivated his team.
He stood six feet, four inches tall and weighed 215 pounds.
While this stature is normal for a quarterback, back then
it was unusual for the signal caller to be that big.

The first quarter was scoreless as both teams tried to
feel each other out for strengths and weaknesses. The Beavers struck first when Doug McDougal caught a 5-yard
pass from Paul Brothers. The Maize and Blue had some
issues getting the offense moving, but on the third possession in the second quarter, it found what it needed.
Running back Mel Anthony bolted for an 84-yard run for
a touchdown that cut the lead 7–6.

On Michigan's next drive, Carl Ward scored on a
43-yard run, and the Wolverines had a 12–6 advantage at

the half. The third and fourth quarters were all Michigan. Anthony scored on runs of 1 and 8 yards, and Timberlake added a 24-yard run to put the game out of reach. Timberlake finished the game seven of ten passing with 77 yards and 57 yards on the ground. Anthony was selected as the game MVP.

The Rose Bowl win snapped a fourteen-year postseason drought for the Wolverines. Although Anthony shone bright that day, it was Timberlake's leadership that boosted Michigan's confidence to win. He had guided the team to a 1964 Big Ten title and now to Rose Bowl victory. He was a first team All-American selection and won the Silver Football Trophy as the MVP of the conference in 1964.

Over his three years in Ann Arbor, he gained 315 yards rushing and three for 1,507 yards in the air. He was responsible for nineteen touchdowns and contributed with six field goals and 36 extra points. He was a valuable member of the team and showed his versatility to score a variety of ways to help the Wolverines win.

Timberlake's dynamic leadership qualities continued after college as he became an ordained Presbyterian minister and was outspoken about his faith. He became active in charitable causes and donated his time and money to help those around him.

What does your reputation say about you? Do people think highly of you? Are they happy to see you and glad you are a part of the team?

PREPARE FOR THE GAME

Perhaps you are at a point in your life where it is important what people think about you. Maybe you want to move up in the corporate world or settle down and start a family. Or maybe circumstances in your life have beckoned you to make some personal changes. Growing up and maturing is a part of life. But no matter what has happened, you are beginning to examine your reputation and what others think about you. Your name can open doors and shut them at the same time. Be careful.

EXECUTE THE PLAY

There is never a wrong time to work on your image. Just be aware it may take some time if improvements are needed. You can't expect people to change their opinions of you overnight. But there are some things you can do to let them know you want to make the switch.

Go at a moderate pace and stick with your desire to do good deeds. Keep your word and do what you say you will do. Go out of your way to help others. Timberlake volunteered for Habitat for Humanity. Find a cause that interests you, become involved, and stick with the plan. Don't be a person who shows up only when it's convenient. Do more than is expected and represent what you stand for in a professional way. Make a good appearance in public and be observant of your body language. What you do when no one is watching speaks volumes about your character. Always act with integrity, smile, and laugh.

Timberlake's status struck fear into his opponents. His daunting stature combined with his determination was a winning combination for Michigan. You may not be a towering person physically, but you can stand head and shoulders above others with your acts of kindness. Go Blue!

What can you do to improve your reputation?

_____
_____
_____
_____
_____
_____
_____
_____
_____
_____
_____
_____
_____
_____
_____
_____
_____
_____
_____
_____
_____
_____
_____
_____
_____
_____
_____
_____
_____
_____

KICK CANCER

Cyle Young

September 2, 2002: Washington at Michigan

IT'S NOT OFTEN THAT A kicker's name becomes commonplace in a fan's home. But kicker Phil Brabbs would be the talk of the town after the 2002 University of Washington game.

Late in the fourth quarter, University of Michigan was down 29–28. Brabbs had missed two field goal attempts during the game, and in the fourth quarter he was temporarily replaced by kicker Troy Nienberg. With 1:24 left in the game, Nienberg missed a go-ahead field goal. Washington took possession on their 20-yard line, but the Michigan defense forced a three-and-out. After the Huskies' punt, Michigan took over possession at its own 42.

Michigan would manage to move the ball up the field, but with six seconds to go, they had managed to get the ball just over midfield. They'd need a miracle Hail Mary pass or one of the longest field goals in their team's history—59 yards—to win the game.

But a substitution penalty on the Washington defense gave the Wolverines a chance. The penalty moved the ball

15 yards closer and gave the Wolverines one final chance at a field goal with five seconds left in the game. The only problem was Michigan had missed three field goals on the day, by two different kickers.

Michigan coach Lloyd Carr chose to send his starting kicker, Phil Brabbs, back into the game to attempt a 44-yard field goal. Brabbs, a former walk-on, had everything to win and everything to lose with this one kick. He lined up for the kick and, in front of 11,491 fans, sent the ball right through the middle of the goalposts for a Michigan win.

The team charged the field in celebration. The number ten Wolverines had won a last-second upset over number nine Washington.

"I didn't know how to react," Brabbs later said. "I started doing circles around the field, then I got tackled by one of my teammates. Then I had ten guys on top of me, then everybody piled on and I got scrunched." This game-winning kick was one of the greatest moments in his Michigan career.

Six years later, Brabbs was visiting his old college stomping grounds when he felt a sharp pain in his foot. He'd later learn at the University Hospital that he had a pulmonary embolism. In 2007, the pain returned to his leg; this time he learned he had multiple myeloma, a rare white blood cell cancer. The diagnosis was devastating. Multiple myeloma was a disease that typically affected people who were sixty-five and older. Brabbs was only 28. But he knew he could beat it. He would kick cancer.

Phil started a blog called *Cancer Kicker* and chronicled his struggles with the disease and his seven rounds of chemotherapy. Through all his adversity, Brabbs shared encouragement and kept a positive look on the situation.

He shared some insight on his thoughts during a talk with the Michigan football team. "Adversity teaches character—that the tough times are when you learn what you're all about." It was one of the many lessons he'd learned as a football player for Coach Carr.

As of the writing of this book, Phil Brabbs is cancer free. He is thankful every day for the time that he still has and continues to have a positive outlook on life and overcoming the adversities he has faced with his health. At diagnosis, one in three people lives past five years with multiple myeloma. Brabbs continues to beat the odds, and he knows that every day is a gift from God.

STAND UP AND FACE IT

In life, you will always face times of adversity, just like Brabbs in the Washington game after missing two previous field goal attempts, and in life, like a rare cancer diagnosis out of the blue. Life will throw you curveballs, and how you handle them will say a lot about your character. You will learn what you are capable of when you face whatever comes against you.

DON'T BACK DOWN

Have you ever experienced multiple failures and just given up? Don't quit. Get back in the game and kick the winning field goal. Who cares about your previous misses, mistakes, or failures? All that people will remember is if you got back in the game and put the ball through the goalposts when the game was on the line. They will forgive your other misses and will celebrate your newfound success with you. Go Blue!

What tests of character have you already faced? What did you find out about yourself from them?

_____

_____

_____

_____

_____

_____

_____

_____

_____

_____

_____

_____

_____

_____

_____

_____

_____

_____

_____

_____

_____

_____

_____

_____

_____

_____

_____

_____

_____

_____

BE WILLING TO CHANGE POSITIONS

Del Duduit

November 11, 1967: Michigan 21, Illinois 14

TOM CURTIS WAS A TALENTED athlete and a high school standout as a quarterback. When he came to University of Michigan in 1966, he was a signal caller on the freshman squad. But the next year, the coaching staff asked him to switch from quarterback on offense to the safety spot on defense.

This is quite an adjustment to make. When an athlete is a quarterback, he is usually one of the most talented players on the team and has a high level of skill and intelligence. Field generals possess a large amount of confidence in their ability and are regarded as leaders on the squad. When Curtis was asked to switch positions, there may have been some initial hesitation on his part. After all, many quarterbacks love the position and feel they are there for a reason. But coaches noticed his ability and felt he could be valuable on the field for the defensive unit. They had chosen Dick Vidmer as starting quarterback and felt Curtis could benefit the team in another position. It seemed a waste to have him on the bench. So he made some mental adjustments, put his ego in check, and made the move.

On November 11, 1967, Curtis made three interceptions against Illinois at safety and helped the Wolverines upset Illinois 21–14. He was the bright spot on a bleak season that saw the Maize and Blue finish 4–6. His three picks tied the Michigan single game record for the most interceptions.

During the 1967 season, Curtis posted seven interceptions and tied the Big Ten Conference record. The next year, he was awarded the Frederick C. Matthaei Award for the best sportsmanship both on and off the field. In 1969, he was an All-American at Michigan, and over his three years at safety, he broke school records for interceptions in a game, season, and career. All still stand today.

What would have happened if he had refused to change positions? The coaches saw potential in Curtis and utilized his talents in a better way. Are you open to change? Are you willing to switch for the betterment of the team?

LOOK OVER THE DEFENSE

Just because you have always done something the same way does not make it the most efficient way of doing things. Can you make improvements, or do you think you are perfect? Perhaps your attitude can stand an adjustment at times. Maybe your boss assigns a task that you feel is beneath you. Or perhaps you did not receive the promotion you thought you deserved. What about your personal life? Are there areas where you could change and improve? Everyone gets into a rut at times, but you must recognize your potential, make necessary changes, and adapt to circumstances.

MAKE THE MOVE

Change can be difficult, especially once you are set in your ways. But adapting to life's circumstances will help you to grow as an individual. Have confidence in yourself, but take responsibility for your actions, and never make excuses when things don't go as planned. You must practice the art of forgiveness, which can be a tough challenge. But you must let go of anger and bitterness so it doesn't hold you down. Instead, be honest and direct with people and offer to help when you see someone struggle. Listen more than you talk, and be open to suggestions. Always maintain a calm and polite demeanor and hold strong to your personal convictions. When you are asked to consider a different perspective, examine the situation and weigh the pros and cons.

Curtis put aside his ego and made the switch for the betterment of the team. He could have stayed at quarterback and not been used to his full potential. Instead, he listened to his coaches and learned a new position that was obviously the right move for all parties involved. Go Blue!

What three things can you change about yourself to improve?

_____

_____

_____

_____

_____

_____

_____

MEECHIGAN

Cyle Young

October 27, 1979: Indiana at Michigan Revisited

ON ONE OF THE MOST famous plays in Michigan football history—John Wangler's last-second touchdown pass to Anthony Carter—legendary Michigan football broadcaster Bob Ufer made his most famous call: "Carter scores! Carter scores! Look at those Wolverines. Ninety-five Wolverines going in the end zone. Carter caught the pass, Indiana is done. Ufer is going out of his mind. I have never seen anything like this in all my forty years of covering Michigan football. Anthony Carter, the human torpedo, caught the pass. Bo Schembechler is looking up at Fielding H. Yost in football's Valhalla, and Bo Schembechler says, 'Thank you, Fielding Yost, thank you, Fielding Yost, for that one.'" Ufer's elation was obvious.

The Wolverines stormed back on a miracle of a play to win the game. At that point in his broadcasting career, Ufer had called 347 football games, but the Anthony Carter catch was the single greatest moment he'd ever witnessed. He continued on, almost on the verge of tears,

"I hope you can hear me, because I have never been so happy."

Ufer wasn't a stranger to Michigan success. He played on the 1939 Wolverine team, but he made his real impact at Michigan as a track star in 1942. Bob Ufer set an indoor world record of 48.1 seconds in the 440-yard dash. He was a three-time Big Ten Conference champion in the 440-yard dash. He loved his university, and he loved Michigan football.

Starting in 1945, Ufer became the lead broadcaster for Michigan football, a job he would continue until his death from cancer thirty-six years later. Bo Schembechler said of Ufer's Anthony Carter touchdown call, "There is only one man that could adequately describe that play, and that's Bob Ufer."

Ufer is still known for the amazing calls of some of Michigan's best highlights. He coined the term *Meechigan* because of his unusual pronunciation of the word *Michigan*. During his game broadcasts, Ufer was unashamedly pro-Michigan. He openly rooted for his Wolverines while he called the game. "Michigan football is a religion," he once said, "and Saturday's the holy day of obligation."

His exuberant style of play-calling has oft been repeated but never replicated with the same kind of passion and tenacity. Bob Ufer was one of the great Michigan Men, and his memory lives on in the hearts and minds of the Michigan faithful.

EMBRACE YOUR "RELIGION"

For Bob Ufer, Michigan football was his religion, his passion, and the thing that made him want to wake up every day. But what's your "religion"? Your passion? What drives and motivates you? Maybe it's Michigan football, your job, kids, wife, or a hobby. Maybe it is actually the religion that you practice. Whatever you find sacred says a lot about who you are and the drive you have to accomplish your goals in life. But you must ensure that your goals line up with your passion, or you will find yourself frustrated, stressed, and burned out.

Does Ufer's story relate to your life in any way? What do you hold sacred?

FIND YOUR PASSION

Do you have an Ufer-like passion about anything in your life? Is there anything that brings you the same kind of joy, spurs your heart onward, or helps you wake up in the morning? For Bob Ufer, that was Michigan football. But what is it for you? Invest your time and attention in something bigger than yourself and watch what happens to your motivation for life. You will find your passion grows and your heart gets compelled to participate in a bigger cause. Go Blue!

What are you passionate about? Or what can you become more passionate about?

_____

_____

_____

_____

_____

_____

_____

_____

—∿—

DEFY THE ODDS AND WIN

Del Duduit

November 13, 1999: Michigan 31, Penn State 27

PENN STATE HAD A LOT riding on the game. The number six ranked Nittany Lions were 9–1 and had national championship aspirations. All they had to do was knock off number sixteen ranked University of Michigan (7–2) and then Michigan State for a potential title game appearance. They were fresh off a loss to University of Minnesota while the Wolverines were riding high after a blowout win over Northwestern University.

Happy Valley was ready for joy once again. But Tom Brady had other plans. With 9:44 to play in the contest, Michigan trailed 27–17. The outcome looked bleak for the Maize and Blue.

Brady, who finished the matchup seventeen of thirty-six for 256 yards and two touchdowns, knew the odds were not in his team's favor. He drove the Wolverines down the field, plunged into the end zone from 5 yards out with 3:26 to go in the fourth quarter, and pulled to within 3 points. Michigan's defense stiffened, and the offense got the ball back with little time left on the game clock.

Brady once again orchestrated a drive and found wide receiver Marcus Knight for an 11-yard touchdown. With 1:46 to play in the game, they had a 31–27 lead. Penn State had time left and drove the ball down the field. They knew how important a win would be for their postseason hopes.

The Nittany Lions reached the Michigan 25-yard line. They could still manage a victory. But all hope was gone after Michigan linebacker Ian Gold forced a fumble by quarterback Kevin Thompson, and the Wolverines went on to pull off the upset and win the game.

Michigan would go on and defeat Ohio State and University of Alabama to win the Orange Bowl, while Penn State dropped the next game to Michigan State, settling for the Alamo Bowl title.

With the odds stacked against Michigan, Brady led back-to-back scoring drives in hostile territory to find triumph.

Have you been in similar situations and felt hopeless? How were you able to pull out the win?

DEVELOP A GAME-WINNING STRATEGY

Circumstances in life can make you feel like you are 10 points behind with only a few minutes to play. Perhaps you have just received notification from your company that you are being transferred. Or maybe you were blindsided with some unanticipated bad news or are facing a health or personal challenge. No one likes to lose or fall behind in the score. When you are looking defeat in the eyes, you must reach down and find the mental stamina and character to go for the win. You must reach deep within and find the determination to continue.

PULL OFF THE UPSET

The most important thing to remember is to never give up. With this in mind, there are some steps to take in order to give yourself a better chance of doing the unthinkable. Distance yourself from drama. In difficult and challenging times, emotions can run high and might provoke a negative reaction. Distractions are not welcome.

Step back and examine your situation. On each play, Brady had to evaluate the defense, make adjustments, and find the open receivers. You must take the same approach. Each play will look different and will require audibles at the line of scrimmage. You also should display confidence in your own ability and decision-making process. This can come about only through daily preparation and personal motivation. Maintain a positive perspective, but always go with your gut and initial reactions to circumstances. Remain focused on the task at hand, and never assume what might happen. Brady knew he had to win each down in order to find the end zone. Each move is important in the big game of life. Take each down with importance, and know that small gains can lead to the go-ahead score.

Brady had the fortitude, coaching, and support of his team to find the will to win. He knew he could not do it alone, but he led the charge. When you show leadership and integrity, your team will follow you into battle. Defy the odds and pull off the upset for a win. Go Blue!

What situations hold you back, and how can you improve them?

HAIL, YES!

Cyle Young

November 22, 1997: Ohio State at Michigan

DEFENSE WINS CHAMPIONSHIPS. THIS ADAGE will always reign true, even in the era of modern touchdowns and air-raid offenses. When a defense can hold its own against an overpowered offense, good things happen. And that's just what the University of Michigan learned in its game against the Ohio State Buckeyes in 1997.

Michigan gained only 189 offensive yards during the rivalry contest. That total was well below its season's average—the Wolverines were averaging over 350 yards offensive per game. But defense and special teams would carry Michigan through the four quarters.

Both teams held each other scoreless in the first quarter, but the Wolverines found steam in the second quarter and opened a 7–0 lead on an Anthony Thomas touchdown run. Michigan quarterback Brian Griese connected with potential Heisman Trophy candidate Charles Woodson for a 37-yard reception on the drive. In the next possession, Michigan held Ohio State to a three-and-out. Woodson received the punt at his team's own 22-yard line before racing up the left sideline for another Michigan touchdown.

And then it happened.

Woodson strutted through the end zone before flashing the famous Heisman Trophy pose. As the leading candidate in the country, the pose was appropriate. It brought flashbacks of Desmond Howard's same punt-return touchdown pose years before. And Woodson made sure to do it right in front of the television cameras. This was his year, and he was without a doubt the best player in the country.

After a blocked extra point, Michigan went into the locker room with a halftime lead, 13–0. On Ohio State's first drive of the second half, they drove deep into Michigan territory, all the way to the Michigan 7. Buckeye quarterback Stanley Jackson tossed a pass into the middle of the end zone, but cornerback Charles Woodson was there to intercept his pass. It was Woodson's seventh interception of the season.

The Wolverines couldn't manage to turn the turnover into points, instead going three-and-out on their own 20. Ohio State took possession after a punt, but on the next play, Michigan's Andre Weathers intercepted another Jackson pass, this time returning it 43 yards for a Michigan touchdown.

With a 20–0 lead late in the fourth quarter, Michigan looked well in control. But two costly fumbles gave the Buckeyes excellent field position. They wouldn't waste the opportunities. Converting both for easy touchdowns, Ohio State clawed back to a 6-point deficit.

Both heavyweight teams held each other on each of the successive drives. Four punts later, the Buckeyes gained possession for what would be their last drive of the game. But four plays brought no yardage, and linebackers Ian Gold and Sam Sword knocked down the Buckeyes' last pass of the game to seal the win.

Too many times in Michigan's history, an end-of-season Ohio State loss upended the Wolverines' hopes and dreams, but not in 1997. The Michigan defense held strong, sending them to the Rose Bowl and the eventual national championship.

Do you let past losses define you? Or are you able to rely on your defense, overcome those losses, and realize your dreams?

PUSH FOR THE WIN

Sometimes life is like that for us all: we need one aspect of our personality or ability to carry us through specific situations. You can't always be everything to everybody. Sometimes you have to find a way to have success, even if it means you have to buckle down and pull one out with a lesser-used aspect of yourself.

Don't be afraid to push yourself a little harder. Sometimes when you do, you discover amazing new things about yourself.

PLAY TO YOUR STRENGTHS

Your unique strengths and hidden talents are the best part of you. There is no one else like you, and that is always to your advantage. Don't play the negative comparison game. It's a mental and emotional trap that keeps you from reaching your fullest potential. Like any athlete, you have to play to your strengths. Once you know what makes you special, use those skills and abilities to your advantage. Tom Brady didn't dance ballet—he was a quarterback. Charles Woodson didn't play offensive tackle; his size and talent made him a playmaker. You need to be exactly who you were created to be and play to your strengths. When you do that, you will accomplish great things on your path to personal victory. Go Blue!

What are your hidden strengths? How can you use them to pull off a win?

_____
_____
_____
_____
_____
_____
_____
_____
_____
_____
_____
_____
_____
_____
_____
_____
_____
_____
_____
_____
_____
_____

BELIEVE IN YOUR TEAM

Del Duduit

November 20, 1999: Michigan 24, Ohio State 17

FOR A FEW MOMENTS, OHIO State fans thought their team was going to pull off the upset.

The number seventeen ranked Ohio State Buckeyes had the number ten ranked University of Michigan Wolverines down in the score in the fourth quarter. But Tom Brady picked up where he had left off the previous week when he guided Michigan to a dramatic comeback over Penn State. This time, archrival Ohio State felt the sting in Ann Arbor.

The Maize and Blue made the most of three Buckeye turnovers in the second half. Two picks and a fumble turned into 17 points for Michigan. DeWayne Patmon had the first interception off OSU quarterback Steve Bellisari early in the third quarter. It was his eighth pick of the season, and he returned it 32 yards to the Buckeye 23 and set up a Hayden Epstein field goal.

Later in the quarter, linebacker Ian Gold took a Bellisari pass back to the Ohio State 8-yard line. On the next play, Michigan scored a touchdown and tied the game at

17 when Brady connected with tight end Shawn Thompson in the end zone.

The Wolverines took the lead after James Whitley forced a fumble, and they took possession on their own 23-yard line. That was when Brady took over and drove his squad 77 yards for the game's winning touchdown. The quarterback found Marquise Walker for a 10-yard score with 5:01 to play in the game. The touchdown was Brady's second in sixteen minutes, and it led his Wolverines away from the potential upset from the team down south.

On the day, Brady was seventeen of twenty-seven in the air for 150 yards and two touchdowns. He believed in his teammates and their ability to come from behind for the win. Just like in life, everyone on the team contributed to the victory. The defense came up with big plans and made sure that Brady and the offense had the ball to score. But in the end, Brady had to believe in his ability to orchestrate the drive. His actions motivated others to do their jobs and work as a team to achieve the big triumph.

What about you? Do your actions help those around you become better? Do you lend a hand and lead the team, or are you content to sit on the bench?

LOOK OVER THE PLAYBOOK

Everyone faces challenges and struggles in life. You are not exempt from this list. Circumstances can alter plans and make you go in a different direction. Your projections may not turn out like you expected. But you have to overcome obstacles and manage to find success and happiness.

Perhaps you know someone who has not risen to the challenge. Maybe a colleague is going through a personal crisis or has a health concern. Perhaps they have been penalized and backed up 15 yards, and they face a fourth down. These instances take place every day in the lives of people around us. But many will not talk to others about their problems. But somehow, you find out about it from a friend or a post on social media. What do you do?

MAKE THE GAME-WINNING DRIVE

There are several things you can do to help someone during a time of trouble. You want to assist but don't want to bail them out of a predicament because they need to learn to survive on their own. But there are some actions you can take to help get them through a bad situation.

You can be encouraging. A simple text message can brighten anyone's day. Reflect on your own hard times and how good it felt when someone sent you a hopeful note. When you offer a positive word, you can lift the spirits of the person on the other end more than you realize. Be an encourager and not an enabler.

You can also acknowledge the good people do. Tell them about their positive qualities and talents. Challenge them to overcome their obstacles and remind them to ignore negative comments or thoughts.

One of the best ways to be of help is to listen. Don't ask questions, but give them time to vent and describe their emotions. Listening is a powerful tool that can help a person heal. Hearing a person out also shows you believe in them enough to give the most valuable asset you own—your time.

Take a moment to encourage and be a positive member of your team. Set the standard and be a source of inspiration to those around you. Go Blue!

How do you encourage others?

_____

_____

_____

_____

_____

_____

_____

_____

_____

_____

_____

_____

_____

_____

_____

_____

_____

_____

_____

_____

_____

_____

_____

_____

—ᴍ—

THE PERFORMANCE

Cyle Young

November 22, 1997: Syracuse at Michigan

IN 1998, DONOVAN MCNABB AND the Syracuse University Orangemen rolled into Ann Arbor as underdogs. Scheduled for what presumably was an easy early season victory for the University of Michigan Wolverines, Syracuse was expected to just be a speed bump on Michigan's road to another Big Ten title.

But Donovan McNabb wasn't a patsy. Michigan quarterback Tom Brady and Syracuse quarterback McNabb would go on to play each other many times in the NFL. Brady would often get the best of those results, but in 1998, in their first meeting, McNabb would leave the day victorious.

McNabb led his team down the field for a score on the first drive of the game. Brady would later remark every time the Orangeman snapped the ball, it seemed as though they'd pick up 10 more yards. McNabb was unstoppable. He would dance and spin and then dance and spin some more. The Michigan defenders couldn't tackle him, let alone touch him. When they got close enough, McNabb would rip off another pass completion. He went 21–27 on the day for 233 yards and added 60 yards rushing.

Coach Bo Schembechler was heard saying that was the single greatest performance he had ever seen by a visiting quarterback at Michigan Stadium. He wasn't wrong. McNabb looked like a man playing against boys.

The Orangemen pounded the Michigan defense, opening up a 24–0 lead. Michigan would cut the lead by seven going into halftime. Syracuse added two touchdowns in the third quarter, embarrassing the Wolverines at home 38–7. Michigan would score 21 points to end the game against Syracuse reserves; the final score was much closer than the actual gameplay. Had McNabb remained in the game, the loss would have been even more legendary.

Michigan had a wake-up call to start the season. They suffered two upset losses after winning the national title. If they wanted to compete in the Big Ten Conference, they had to get their act together.

And that's just what they did. Michigan rolled through the next eight games. Posting an 8–0 record, they held six opponents under 10 points. The team would go on to claim a share of the Big Ten title, but not without experiencing a rough start to the season.

How do you react when you get off to a difficult start? Are you able to push forward and eventually bring the win home?

DON'T GET BLINDSIDED

Ever had a job like that? At first it was extremely difficult, even though you'd thought it would be easy. Maybe you experienced early turmoil when you'd expected a much easier landing. What about a relationship or marriage? Did you expect it to be easier to connect, communicate, and get along, only to find out it's much more difficult and complex than you ever imagined?

You can turn it all around. The Wolverines did, even after they were thoroughly embarrassed by one of the greatest quarterbacks of all time. But it took a new attitude and a new ferocity during the post-Syracuse practices to wake the Wolverines up.

MAKE PRACTICE CHANGES

Are there changes you can make to your practice schedule? Do you need to wake up in your workplace or relationships? Making healthy changes is part of reaching your full potential at work, home, or play. If you want to improve your performance, it may start with doing the little things right. Show up to work on time. Stay late. Put on a smile and be a better coworker, friend, or family member. A kind heart and positive attitude are contagious. Help others and put them first and watch the ripple effect around you. Be the change you want to see. Go Blue!

Make a list of some of the changes you can make in your work or life to help you have the success that you want to have in life. And then make sure to apply the adjustments.

_____

_____

_____

_____

_____

_____

BE VERSATILE IN EVERYTHING YOU DO

Del Duduit

David Baas: Offensive Lineman 2001–2004

DURING HIS TENURE AT THE University of Michigan, David Baas became known as one of the best offensive linemen in the storied history of the Maize and Blue. He started his career at left guard but moved over to the center position his senior year. This was not an easy switch to make, especially since he had played the same position for three years.

An offensive lineman must be able to adapt, but to effectively go from one position to another is a substantial move. The role is quite simple, but the job description can be tedious. Linemen are the strength and backbone of the team's plays on offense. They protect the quarterback and running backs by blocking the defenders. Their mission is to pave the way for the ball carriers to reach the end zone, and they accept the responsibility without fanfare or glory.

Baas did this well his first three seasons in Ann Arbor. Then midway through his final year, he was moved to center. Although these two positions are only three feet apart on the line, a center has much more responsibility. Baas's new role was to snap the ball to the quarterback and be the line general. He accepted the new assignment and excelled. He was a consensus All-American and the co-winner of the Remington Trophy, which is awarded to the best center in the nation. Baas also earned the Hugh H. Rader Award, which is an honor given to the best offensive lineman at Michigan.

He showed his willingness to accept a new role for the betterment of the team. He demonstrated his versatility, put his ego aside, and did what was best for the squad. As a finalist for the Outland Trophy his senior year, he was drafted into the NFL in 2005 early in the second round by the San Francisco Giants.

The Wolverines have featured many outstanding linemen over the years, but few have shown the flexibility and selflessness that Baas did. His legacy is pure teamwork.

What is your legacy? Are you able to put the good of those around you before your own interests?

BE WILLING TO CHANGE

It's fair to describe Baas this way: He was unselfish because he preferred to stay in the trenches and pave the way for his teammates to excel. He liked to sacrifice for the betterment of his team. Does this describe you? Would you be happy if a coworker received all the glory and praise for your hard work? This can be a challenge for anyone. Are you willing to work behind the scenes to make sure your teammates reach the goal line? Does public recognition matter, or are you content knowing your team got the job done? These are hard questions to answer.

Everyone enjoys a little limelight if it's deserved. But are you willing to take a back seat for someone else to prosper?

LEAD THE WAY

Baas received his fair share of notoriety during his four years at Michigan. But he gladly took on a new role and performed well when asked for the sake of the team. He did such a great job that he was honored for his work. But the switch did not come without sacrifice. You may have changes in your life that also require giving up some things. You may need to make adjustments, starting with your attitude.

One way you can check your outlook is to make it a habit to perform random acts of kindness for others. What if you smiled at a stranger every day or said "good morning" to someone you don't know? This could create a chain reaction and lead other people to do the same thing. Earmark a portion of your check to go to charity, and volunteer to work with people who are less fortunate.

Make it a point to demonstrate patience in everyday situations. Today, so many people become frustrated by having to wait in a checkout line or wait on the driver in front of them to move quickly when the traffic light turns green. We live in an era of instant gratification, which fuels impatience. If you have to wait on something, it's going to be okay. Treat others the way you wish to be treated, and don't stress when things don't go exactly the way you want.

Maybe you have been promoted at work or you are a new father. You will have new responsibilities. Are you ready to put your pride aside, take on a new role, and excel at it? Success doesn't always come in an instant, and you have to make sure your attitude is right. Go Blue!

How can you take on new roles in life?

FIRST GAME

Cyle Young

May 30, 1879: Racine vs. Michigan

THE UNIVERSITY OF MICHIGAN, THE winningest football program in college football history, began its football adventure with a 1–0 victory over Racine College.

The Purple Stockings from Racine had issued a challenge to Michigan. Their challenge was posted in a fall 1878 issue of the *Chronicle*, which at the time was a weekly newspaper at the University of Michigan. Racine offered to meet the Wolverines on the field in Chicago, and they offered Michigan two-thirds of the gate receipts for coming to play.

Michigan had a football association at the time, but they didn't have a twenty-two-member team to participate in the contest. Three weeks after the letter was posted in the *Chronicle*, the Michigan Football Association met to discuss the challenge. They accepted Racine's challenge, and the game would take place the next spring.

Twenty-seven days before the game, the association met to select the twenty-two players who'd represent the university. There wouldn't be much time to practice the sport, which was still quite new, but the Wolverines would at least field a team.

Five hundred spectators showed up to watch the spectacle. The game consisted of two innings. During the first inning, the teams held each other scoreless, although Michigan had a touchdown canceled on a referee's controversial decision. Michigan dominated the second inning. For most of the period, the ball hovered around the Racine goal, until finally Michigan kicker and team captain David DeTarr converted a placekick for the game's only score.

The *Chicago Daily Tribune* dubbed the game "the first rugby-football game to be played west of the Alleghenies." Racine College went on to play football for the next decade, but a decline in enrollment in the college ultimately led to the discontinuation of the sport. Michigan, on the other hand, went on to become one of the most respected and feared football teams in the country.

Even though it took them a little while, Michigan responded to the Racine challenge. And when they responded, they did so in a resounding way—with a win.

How do you respond to challenges in your life? Do you take time to process the costs and conditions, or do you lash out quick in defense?

SLOW YOUR ROLL

When you are challenged by someone—a friend, neighbor, coworker, employer, whomever—take time to process and think *before* you respond. Your decisions will be better, your temperament will be more controlled, and your results will improve. Resist lashing out in anger or frustration, and instead take a more controlled and logical approach. You'll be happier and less stressed, and you will have a better chance of coming up with a successful and possibly victorious response to the challenge.

RISE TO THE CHALLENGE

Better decisions start with better thinking. But once you've got a clear head, you have to create a good plan. Create a step-by-step checklist and chart your next actions. Find satisfaction by accomplishing each smaller step toward your bigger goal and don't be afraid to fail. Challenges will come, but those hurdles can also make you stronger and more resilient. When you reach your final destination, you will be transformed by the process, but those changes will make reaching your goal all that more rewarding. Go Blue!

What are some challenges you've faced in your life? What were your reactions to them, both good and bad?

_____

_____

_____

_____

_____

_____

_____

_____

_____

_____

_____

_____

_____

USE YOUR UNIQUE ABILITY

Del Duduit

October 31, 1987: Michigan 29, Northwestern 6

MARK MESSNER DID NOT LET his small size limit his ability on the field of play.

He was six feet, three inches tall, which is not exactly little, but it's a bit short for a defensive lineman. To make up for his limitation in stature, he used intelligence and speed to counter his opponents. Messner became a "Dennis the Menace" to quarterbacks, and offensive linemen could not keep up with his speed. He outsmarted the men on the other side of the line of scrimmage and enjoyed playing the game of cat and mouse.

He was described as a matador who stepped around the bull and teased those trying to block him. Messner combined youthful intensity and intelligence to make the big plays on defense for Michigan. He was a redshirt freshman who played in all twelve games in 1985, a year when Michigan finished 10–1 and ranked number two in the final AP Poll. He set a team record with eleven sacks and had seventy-one tackles.

In the Fiesta Bowl, Messner was named Defensive Player of the Game in the 27–23 win over Nebraska. His sophomore year, he was named to the All-Big Ten Team for the second year in a row. Then, on October 31 in his junior season, Messner set a single-game record when he sacked the Northwestern quarterback five times. For the season, he had eleven total sacks and was selected by the *Sporting News* as a first-team defensive lineman on the 1987 All-American Team. His teammates at Michigan also voted him as the defensive player of the year.

Messner's senior year was spectacular. He led a defense that spearheaded a 10–0 Michigan run after losing the first two regular season games. The Wolverines won the coveted Rose Bowl by beating USC 22–14. In that season, Messner had eight sacks and set a school record with twenty-six tackles for a loss. At the end of his final year, he was chosen as a consensus first-team defensive lineman on the All-American Team and played in the Hula Bowl and the Japan Bowl All-Star games. Messner was the first position player in the Big Ten Conference to be chosen as a first-team all-conference in all four years he played. In 2014, he was inducted into the University of Michigan's Athletic Hall of Honor.

At first glance, Messner was thought to be too small to play his position. But his determination to be the best proved to be larger than life.

What about you? Do you let possible limitations hold you back? How can you overcome the odds?

SIZE UP YOUR COMPETITION

Perhaps you are in a situation where people perceive you as having a disadvantage. Maybe you did not finish at the top of your class, or job seekers desire more experience than you have on your résumé. You might even be in a situation where you feel inadequate to get the job done. You may have low self-esteem and feel others have an advantage over you in many areas. The first step in overcoming any obstacle is to realize you are worth more than you think.

CATCH THE OFFENSE OFF GUARD

Messner lacked the size to compete with large offensive linemen, so he used quickness and intelligence to reach his target. You may also have to use other tools in your arsenal to make up for what you don't have. Take inventory of the many positive traits you can utilize to find your success. Create a vision for what you want to accomplish, and use your abilities to your advantage. Be ready to make mistakes and learn from them. Work hard, and maintain a positive attitude.

Accept who you are, and make your play with your own attributes. Don't compromise your convictions to make people want to be around you. Don't let anyone underestimate what you can do, and make sure you believe in yourself. Hone your skills, and use them to sack the quarterback and be the MVP of your own life. Go Blue!

How can you showcase your own unique talents?

_____

_____

_____

_____

_____

_____

THE 100TH GAME

Cyle Young

November 22, 2003: Ohio State at Michigan

IN 2003, OHIO STATE UNIVERSITY met University of Michigan in Ann Arbor for the one hundredth game in their rivalry. Two juggernaut teams would meet on the field once again to determine the conference championship and Bowl Championship Series (BCS) representation. National championship considerations also hung in the balance.

Ohio State held the advantage in the ranking coming into the game. The Buckeyes were ranked number four in the country, while the Wolverines had climbed to a number five ranking.

Michigan took an early 7–0 lead, after the Buckeyes failed to turn an early Michigan turnover into points. The Buckeyes' number one ranked defense struggled to contain Wolverine running back Chris Perry, who rushed for 154 yards and two touchdowns, and wide receiver Braylon Edwards, with seven catches for 130 yards and two touchdowns.

At halftime, the Wolverines were fully in control of the game; their 21–7 lead accurately reflected the play on the field. Michigan received the second-half kick. Quarterback John Navarre led his Wolverines down the field, ending the drive with Perry's first touchdown of the game. But Ohio State wouldn't just give up against their rivals. The conference championship was on the line.

Ohio State took over on the Michigan 33-yard line after a muffed punt by the Wolverines. Four plays later, Buckeye quarterback Craig Krenzel hit receiver Santonio Holmes for a 13-yard touchdown. The Ohio State defense forced Michigan to a three-and-out on the next series, but a majestic punt by the Wolverines pinned the Buckeyes at their own 7-yard line.

Krenzel, the Buckeyes' starting quarterback, had been injured on a previous series, so the drive started with backup quarterback Scott McMullen under center. In ten plays, including a 40-yard reception by Holmes, McMullen drove the team to the Michigan 2-yard line. One play later, running back Lydell Ross punched it in, bringing the score within 7.

Two plays later, Michigan quarterback Navarre was intercepted. All the game's momentum had shifted in the Buckeyes' favor. But a three-play defensive stand gave the Wolverines some much needed breathing room. Navarre quickly led his team down the field for the game's final score.

Late in the fourth quarter, Michigan seemed to be losing grasp of the game. Over the period of a couple minutes, they went from a 21-point lead to being up by only 7 points, with Ohio State in control of the ball after a turnover. At that point, the Wolverines could have given up and let the Buckeyes storm back into the game. Ohio State was the higher-ranked team—no one would blame them for losing, right?

But Michigan held firm. The defense came together and would not allow the Buckeyes to get an important first down. Teammates help each other, and it was the defense's turn to help the offense overcome a costly mistake.

Michigan won the top-five matchup and received an invitation to play number one University of Southern California in the Rose Bowl. They would not win that game, but the bowl loss wouldn't undercut an excellent season.

BE A TEAM PLAYER

Have you ever had to make up for a coworker's mistakes? What about a family member or friend? It's never easy to find yourself in a high-pressure situation, especially one that you didn't cause. But teams come together in times of great difficulty to help each other out. Next time you get put in this awkward position, remember you are an important part of a team, and working together to help others through difficulty is one of the ways that you can realize great success in your life or workplace.

SHIFT THE MOMENTUM

A motivated team can make all the difference in the world. But every team member has to be on the same page. You can't control every person's interactions, but you can influence them by how you present yourself. Have patience with others. Show respect, even when it's not earned. Be kind and gracious. Pull your own weight. It's amazing how far a please and thank you can go to reinforcing relationships. And most importantly, keep your word. Don't let others on you team down. They are counting on you just like you are counting on them. A well-working team can create its own momentum. Go Blue!

Have you ever dropped the ball, so to speak? Have you ever placed your family or coworkers in a difficult situation because you forgot a deadline, missed an appointment, or didn't complete a task? How did you respond, and how did your "teammates" respond to you? Is there anything you wish you could have done differently?

_____

_____

_____

_____

_____

_____

_____

_____

_____

_____

_____

_____

_____

_____

_____

_____

_____

_____

_____

_____

_____

CONCLUSION

Del Duduit

I HOPE THAT OVER THE past fifty-two chapters, you have been inspired by *Michigan Motivations*. We tried to put together a mixture of fond memories of wonderful athletes who made fantastic plays, along with a few history lessons, too. The entire book had one mission: to encourage you in your journey here on earth.

I must admit, this project made me hesitate at first. After all, I am from Ohio. My first book is called *Buckeye Believer: 40 Days of Devotions for the Ohio State Faithful*. But when I had the opportunity to talk about this book in more detail, I knew writing it would be an enjoyable process. I enjoy the rivalry between University of Michigan and Ohio State and appreciate each one's passion.

It was a pleasure to coauthor *Michigan Motivations* with my friend Cyle, who offered a unique perspective because he played for the Maize and Blue. Over the months spent researching this book, I learned a lot about the program.

I enjoy going back in time to find out interesting facts, and this book was no exception. As a former sportswriter and editor working in Southern Ohio, I naturally followed the rivalry that exists between Columbus and Ann Arbor. I have also had the privilege to attend a few games when Michigan rolled into Ohio. There are three memories that stand out.

1. The 2002 game when Ohio State secured the undefeated season and knocked off Michigan 14–9. It was memorable because when my friend Troy and I tried to make our way out of the Horseshoe, we were shoved in a different direction and ended up getting a smell and taste of pepper spray that was used to deter the rush of OSU fans who wanted to tear down the goalposts.

2. I remember that game on November 23 because it was bitter cold. Before the contest, Troy and I were at a canopy tailgating with some friends. Chili at 9 a.m. on a frigid Columbus morning can taste mighty good. But on this particular day, some male supporters from Michigan ran through our tailgating section with shirts off and their chests painted Maize and Blue. Let's just say their language was not warm and friendly. Several cans of soda and whatever else was handy smashed into the young men as they ran through the crowd.

3. I was with my friend Wayne on a bone-chilling day in Columbus when Michigan knocked off the Buckeyes 13–9. It was a struggle to stay warm. Toward the end of the game, a Wolverine fan and a supporter of the Scarlet and Gray let the emotions of the game come to a boil. Words were exchanged—and then punches. They were a few rows in front of us and coming our way. The only thought that ran through my mind was that I was going to have to move, just when I was starting to get

warm. But just when I was about to shift to avoid the altercation, it broke up.

It's funny that the outcomes of the games were not what I remember the most. What stood out to me were circumstances before, during, or after the game. That is how life can be for most of us. Unfortunate circumstances can distract us and leave a negative impression on us. The games I attended were fun, but that's not what comes to my mind when I recall those events.

But my hope is that you have a positive impression of Michigan football, as I do, now that you have flipped through these pages. I hope you have learned important lessons, such as encouragement is important when you are pressed to the limit, and learning from an experience can be the key to success in school, your job, or with your family. Prioritizing your time for what really matters is a lesson we all need to incorporate.

Most athletes will tell you that the game is not as difficult as the practice leading up to it. When it's kickoff time and the ball is in the air, the players tune out everything else around them and become focused on their assignment. They rely on the coaching staff and the studying they have done in preparation for that moment.

The same applies to the game of life. You must prepare for the big moment and make sure you are mentally and physically ready to win each day. There will be moments when you taste defeat, but you must learn from it and get ready for the next game. Life is all about making adjustments and being prepared to defeat your rival.

I hope this book has both given you an insight into the history of Michigan football and encouraged you to do better each day. Don't focus on the negative events that happen around you but instead on your assignment and game plan. Life has its ups and downs, and the easy decision sometimes is to just give up. But football teaches us lessons of perseverance and determination. And I hope *Michigan Motivations* has inspired you as much as it has me.

Make your memories good ones, and don't be afraid to fail. Take chances and execute your game plan. Live the best you can and serve others with a thankful heart.

I am still a Buckeye fan, but writing this book has given me the opportunity to see Michigan football in a new light.

Go Blue!

SOURCES

Chengelis, Angelique S. "UM's Mike Hart Regrets 'Little Brother' Jab at MSU." *Detroit News*. Last modified October 15, 2015. https://www.detroitnews.com/story/sports/college/university-michigan/2015/10/15/hart-little-brother/74027086/.

CHAPTER 8

"Michigan Made 119 Points: Almost Equaled Phenomenal Score against Buffalo Simply Rushed Ball over the Aggie's Line at Will Made Touchdown Oftener Than Once in Two Minutes." *Detroit Free Press*, October 9, 1902.
"The M.A.C. Game." *Michigan Alumnus*, November 1902.

CHAPTER 10

WolverineHistorian. "1979: Michigan vs. Indiana—Carter's Game Winner." Last modified August 8, 2008. Video, 1:31. https://www.youtube.com/watch?v=7M3jVy_kJR4.

CHAPTER 14

Associated Press. "Michigan Finally Wins a Rose Bowl Contest." *Logansport Pharos-Tribune*, January 2, 1981.

Associated Press. "Schembechler Chronology." *Argus-Press,* December 15, 1989.

Associated Press. "Wolverines Want to Win Rose Bowl for Schembechler." *New Mexican,* December 26, 1980.

United Press International. "Schembechler Lets Off Steam." *Valley Independent,* December 31, 1980.

CHAPTER 22

Woolford, Dave. "1950 Snow Bowl: A Game for All Time Frozen in History." *Blade,* November 15, 2000.

Ohio State. "Ohio Stadium Celebrates Its 500th Game Saturday vs. Northwestern." Accessed September 1, 2019. https://ohiostatebuckeyes.com /ohio-stadium-celebrates-its-500th-game-saturday-vs-northwestern/.

CHAPTER 26

Rothstein, Michael. "Carr Recalls First Game at Helm." ESPN. Last modified August 28, 2012. http://www.espn.com/colleges/michigan/football /story/_/id/8310515/michigan-wolverines-remember-last-big -opener.

CHAPTER 32

Jennings, Chantel. "Michigan-ND rivalry's Best Games." ESPN. Last modified September 9, 2011. http://www.espn.com/colleges /michigan/football/story/_/id/6947734/michigan-wolverines -top-games-notre-dame.

CHAPTER 42

Dickson, James. "Former University of Michigan Football Player Philip Brabbs Trying to Kick Cancer." *Ann Arbor News.* Last modified March 1, 2010. http://www.annarbor.com/sports/um-football /former-university-of-michigan-kicker-philip-brabbs-trying-to -kick-cancer.

ESPN. "Brabbs' Last-Second Field Goal Deflates Huskies." Last modified August 31, 2002. http://www.espn.com/college-football/recap? gameId=222430130.

CHAPTER 44

Expressfan. "1979 Michigan Indiana Football - Anthony Carter + Ufer."
Video, 3:39. https://www.youtube.com/watch?v=AEF6edfexco.

Rosenbaum, Mike. "Meechigan Man." *Michigan Today*. Last modified June 2, 2016. https://michigantoday.umich.edu/2016/06/02/meechigan-man/.

CHAPTER 48

Jenkins, Lee. "In '98, McNabb and Syracuse Beat Brady and Michigan." *New York Times*. Last modified February 2, 2005. https://www.nytimes.com/2005/02/02/sports/football/in-98-mcnabb-and-syracuse-beat-brady-and-michigan.html.

CHAPTER 50

Perry, Will. *The Wolverines: A Story of Michigan Football*. Huntsville, AL: Strode Publishers, 1974.

CYLE YOUNG is a Michigan Man who bleeds Maize and Blue. He played on the 1997 University of Michigan national championship football team, and he takes his wife and three children back to see football games each season. During the final two years of his collegiate career, he also participated on the wrestling team.

He is a lead pastor of a church in Michigan and is still married to his college sweetheart, who has blessed him with three wonderful children. Cyle is also a respected literary agent. He has sold more than two hundred of his clients' books to publishing houses and currently represents authors who have combined to sell more than 27 million books.

As an accomplished children's and nonfiction writer in his own right, Cyle has won more than twenty awards for his writing. Quarry Press will be releasing two of Cyle's own upcoming books, *Little Michigan: Small Town Destinations* and *The Buckeye Candy: Ohio's Trademark Dessert*, while Crosslink Publishing will be releasing Cyle's Bible picture book series. You can find out more about Cyle at his website, www.cyleyoung.com.

DEL DUDUIT is a nonfiction author from Lucasville, Ohio. His first book, *Buckeye Believer: 40 Days of Devotions for the Ohio State Faithful*, was a Selah Award finalist at the 2019 Blue Ridge Mountains Christian Writers

Conference. His second book, *Dugout Devotions: Inspirational Hits from MLB's Best*, and his third book, *First Down Devotions: Inspiration from the NFL's Best*, were both released in 2019.

As a former sportswriter, he has won both Associated Press and Ohio Prep Sports writing awards. His weekly blog appears at delduduit.com, and his articles have been published by Athletes in Action, *Clubhouse Magazine*, *Sports Spectrum*, *The Sports Column*, *One Christian Voice*, *The Christian View Online Magazine*, and *Portsmouth Metro Magazine*. His blogs have appeared on *One Christian Voice* and its national affiliates across the country, on ToddStarnes.com (of Fox News), and on *Almost an Author* and *The Write Conversation*.

During the November 2017 Ohio Christian Writers Conference (OCWC), Del was named Outstanding Author and received first place awards in both Short Non-Fiction and Inspirational. At the 2018 OCWC, he received first place for Short Non-Fiction.

He and his wife, Angie, are also the coeditors of *Southern Ohio Christian Voice* (sohiochristianvoice.com). Follow Del on Twitter @delduduit.